Debbie Shore's
SEWING ROOM SECRETS
Quilting

First published in 2020
Search Press Limited
Wellwood, North Farm Road,
Tunbridge Wells, Kent TN2 3DR
United Kingdom

Photograph of the Janome longarm sewing machine on page 13 is used with kind permission from, and remains the copyright of, Janome UK Ltd. For more information on Janome machines, please visit the website: www.janome.co.uk

All remaining photographs by Garie Hind.

Text copyright © Debbie Shore, 2020
Photographs © Garie Hind, 2020
Design copyright © Search Press Ltd., 2020

ISBN: 978-1-78221-547-9

Suppliers
For details of suppliers, please visit the Search Press website: www.searchpress.com

For further inspiration:

– join the Half Yard Sewing Club:
www.halfyardsewingclub.com

– visit Debbie's YouTube channel:
www.youtube.com/user/thimblelane

– visit Debbie's website:
www.debbieshoresewing.com

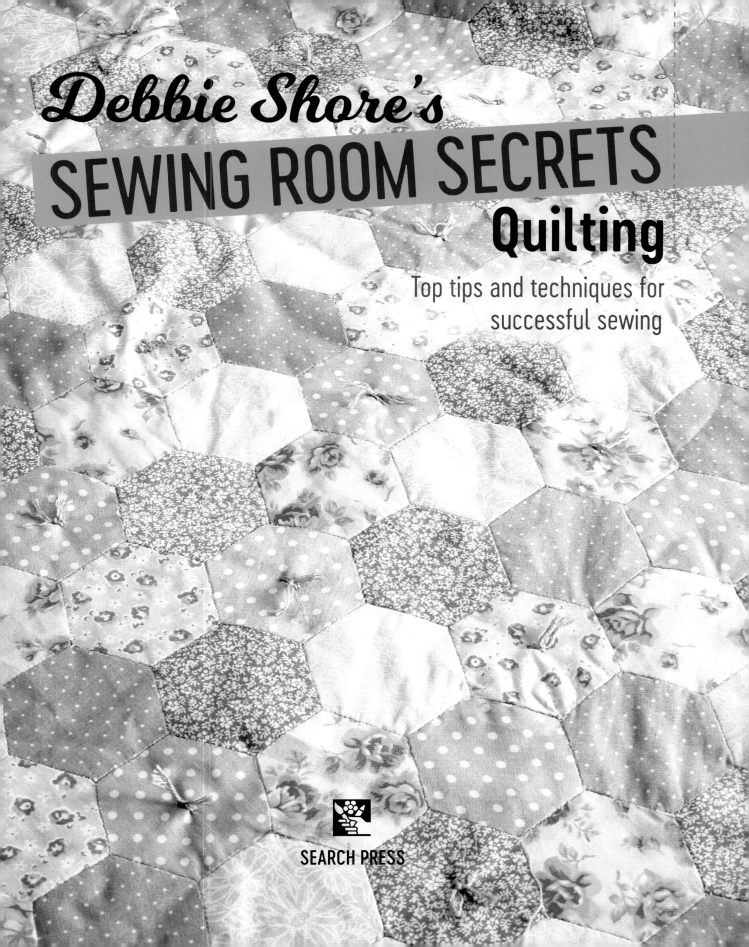

Debbie Shore's
SEWING ROOM SECRETS
Quilting

Top tips and techniques for
successful sewing

SEARCH PRESS

CONTENTS

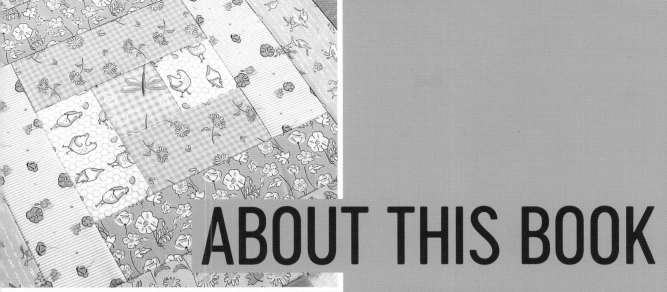

ABOUT THIS BOOK

Take a few stitches through layers of top fabric, some padding and backing fabric and there you go – you're a quilter! Quilting can be a little daunting for many people who are imagining bed-sized quilts, but quilting can be much simpler than this – you can make something as small as an egg cosy and quilt it.

In this book, I'd like to introduce you to a selection of different quilting techniques (both hand-sewn and machine-sewn), explain the difference between patchwork and quilting (although a lot of the time they go hand in hand) and hopefully give you lots of ideas and inspiration through projects you'll find easy to make, but you could re-work and add to if you're a more experienced sewer.

The main thing I'd like to instil in you is the confidence to have a go. Every award-winning quilter started in the same place as you: they made their first cut in their fabric, they sewed their first stitch and they made their first mistake. They are award-winning because they carried on. I'm not suggesting you must head towards competition level! But nobody is born with the ability to sew. You need only to try, practise and enjoy! So go choose your fabric and let's get started!

Debbie x

ABOUT ME

My mum was a seamstress, making clothes for me, my sister and other members of the family, particularly when a wedding was forthcoming! Our house was always busy with fittings; the drawers and cupboards were filled with fabrics; and the sound of sewing machines revving and crisp scissors crunching through layers of fabric is still very nostalgic for me. Sewing was never my intended career, it was more of a hobby and necessity, particularly when I had kids of my own and alterations and repairs were the affordable way of keeping their wardrobes smart and up-to-date!

For over thirty years I have worked as a TV presenter, while still enjoying my sewing hobby in my spare time. A few years ago, several elements of my life started coming together… I made up some cushion covers, and was so pleased with them that I asked my husband Garie, a fashion photographer, to take some pictures. I sent the projects off to Search Press, who produced my first book, *Making Cushion Covers*. This was the first of now twenty-two sewing project books, and my own range of patterns and products.

So now my own cupboards are filled with fabrics and my home has the sound of revving sewing machines and crunching scissors. Who knows, in a few years' time my children may be saying exactly the same thing!

WHAT IS QUILTING?

Quilting is simply the method of stitching three layers of fabric together. This 'sandwich' consists of top and backing fabrics, with a layer of wadding/batting in the centre. The top fabric can be plain, patterned or patchworked. The wadding/batting comes in many thicknesses (referred to as the 'loft'), and can be made from natural or synthetic fibres. More about patchwork and padding later; for now let's take a look at some of the different ways of quilting your project. Remember – that project doesn't have to be a full-sized bed quilt; as a beginner, you may prefer to start with something smaller, such as a placemat (see right) or pillowcase (as seen on page 70).

The appearance of your stitches can be as much a part of your quilt as the colour and pattern of your fabric. Choose contrasting thread to make the stitched design really stand out, or make the stitches less noticeable by 'stitching in the ditch' (sewing over an existing seam) using clear or co-ordinating thread.

In terms of what stitches to use, it is your choice whether to free-motion embroider your quilting design, either freehand or by following existing designs and templates; hand- or machine-sew lines or squares (known as 'cross-hatching') across your fabric; or even tie the layers together with knotted thread, then either make bows or add buttons to embellish.

If you're using a patterned fabric, try outlining elements of the pattern with stitching (which you can see on page 45). If you want a uniform, professional finish to your quilt, or if you find the prospect of quilting a large project a little daunting, take your quilt to a longarm quilting expert – they will have specific machines, a catalogue of designs and a wealth of knowledge that they will share with you!

Covering your work in dense stitches will give a firmer feel to your quilt and is an excellent choice for items that will be laundered, as it will help to keep the layers of fabric from shifting. A looser quilting stitch will create a softer feel to your quilted item. However, it is worth taking note of your wadding/batting manufacturer's guidance on how far apart your stitches should be.

Snowflake Placemat (see page 78).

Humbug Hexie Quilt (see page 90).

Important note

As fabric for quilting and patching is mostly measured and cut using the imperial system, I have used this throughout the book. The imperial measurement is always accompanied by the equivalent metric measurement in parentheses.

WHAT IS PATCHWORK?

Although this book concentrates on quilting techniques, many of you will be quilting patchworked projects so I thought I would give you an overview of a few different techniques.

Patchwork is the method of sewing together small pieces of fabric to create a larger piece. It can make up the top layer of fabric in a quilt, or can be left unquilted to make projects for the home, clothing and other craft items.

Patchwork is a technique that has been around for centuries, serving both decorative and practical purposes. It is decorative as both intricate and simple (and, under these headings, mosaic and illusional) designs can be created through clever use of shapes and colours. Patchwork is practical, too, as scraps of fabric can be re-purposed so as not to waste unwanted or worn-out items of clothing, and – by the same token – could also create memory pieces.

As a beginner, you may wish to start by simply sewing squares of fabric together with colours in no particular order, or organized into a tiled pattern (most of us start our journey with the basic nine-patch block); then, you can move on to half-square and quarter-square triangles, diamonds, hexagons and more of the many geometric shapes traditionally used in patchwork.

Templates are available to help with accurate cutting and fussy cutting, which is a way of placing the template over a specific area of fabric to position the print. For instance, you may like to pick out a flower to place in the centre of a hexagon – special, clear templates allow you to see the flower so you can centralize it before cutting.

Patchwork techniques include hand or machine piecing; English paper piecing (see page 76); foundation piecing, which uses a pre-printed background fabric (see page 43); and crazy patchwork. Large items such as bed quilts are usually broken down into blocks – these are repeatable squares of patchworked pieces arranged either to tessellate or tile across the whole quilt (for examples of this see the Mini Chicken Quilt on page 48 and the Table Runner on page 62), or separated with long strips of fabric that act as borders, known as 'sashing' (see page 66).

While patchwork and quilting do seem to go hand in hand, they are two very different techniques that can be used either together or separately, giving you endless choices of exciting projects to create!

Nine-patch block.

Half-square triangles.

English paper piecing 'jewel' design.

MY QUICK TIPS

A few key sewing tips before you get started...

⊕ Invest in a lint roll, particularly if you're working with fabrics like fleeces, which tend to be magnets for dust, threads and cat hair!

⊕ Stick a tape measure along the front of your cutting table – it's a handy way to measure fabrics.

⊕ Steel wool stuffed inside a pincushion can help keep pins and needles sharp.

⊕ Occasionally cutting through aluminium foil will help to keep your scissors sharp.

⊕ Make the most of wall space: you'll be able to find items quickly, and it helps to keep your work space clear. Many quilters keep a sheet of natural wadding/batting on their wall. Patchwork pieces of fabric will stick to the fibres so that patterns can easily be arranged.

⊕ If you're having problems threading a hand-sewing needle, spray a little hairspray on your fingers and pass the thread through. When it dries, the end of the thread will be stiff enough to thread.

⊕ Use dental floss to hand-sew buttons onto your projects: it's very strong, so you're less likely to lose a button!

⊕ Keep a magnet to hand for when you drop pins and needles on the floor!

⊕ When pinning fabric pieces, pin at a 90-degree angle to the raw edges with the pin heads sitting off the fabric. This way, it's easy to remove the pins as you sew, and if your machine needle accidentally hits a pin it's more likely to roll off it, instead of hitting the top of the pin, which could break your needle.

⊕ Keep your sewing machine manual somewhere accessible. There are usually troubleshooting pages at the back, which may come in handy!

⊕ Make sure there are no little 'nicks' on your thread spool. The thread could catch on these as you sew and may pull or even break your stitches.

⊕ If you find your foot slips off your sewing machine pedal, wrap a couple of elastic bands around it to give your foot a bit of extra grip.

9

Use a lint roll to clean up your fabric.

Cut through foil to keep your scissors sharp.

Use a magnet to pick up dropped needles and pins.

Insert pins at right angles to the fabric so they are easy to remove.

⊕ Not sure which is the right side of plain fabric? Take a look at the selvedge/selvage. The hooks that stretch the fabric in the printing process go through the edges of the fabric from the back to the front, so the front side will have little holes that appear rougher than the back. (See also page 27.)

⊕ When using adhesive sheets with intricate appliqué motifs, scratch the middle of the paper backing with a pin, and remove the backing from the centre. This will stop the paper tugging at the edge of the fabric, which can cause it to fray.

⊕ Mark an accurate seam allowance by tying together two pencils. The distance between the two points will be ¼in (5mm). Pop another pencil in the middle and you'll have a ⅝in (1.5cm) seam allowance.

⊕ Toe separators are a perfect place for storing bobbins!

⊕ Sewing a straight line? Practice makes perfect. In the meantime, use the markings on the needle plate, or try putting masking tape or an elastic band over the bed of your machine and using this as a guide for the edge of your fabric.

⊕ Avoid cutting wadding/batting with a rotary cutter and mat. The fibres of the fabric can be pushed into the cuts on the mat and can then be difficult to remove!

⊕ To prevent your thread from tangling, make sure you thread your needle (hand or machine) in the direction that the thread comes off the spool.

⊕ If you need to lift your sewing machine needle, always turn the hand wheel towards you to help protect the gears and mechanisms inside the machine.

⊕ When sewing seams such as the lining in a bag, I start at the cross section so that I can line the seams up precisely. Nobody notices a perfect seam, but they certainly notice a bad one!

See also the fabric terminology section, on page 27.

Selvedges/selvages tell you which is the front of the fabric.

Toe separators are perfect for storing bobbins.

Start seams at the cross section when sewing lining in a bag.

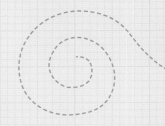

QUILTING
ESSENTIALS

SEWING MACHINE

A sewing machine is probably the most expensive and most important sewing tool you'll buy, so take your time to choose the right model. It should last you for many years to come. There are two main types of machine: electronic and computerized.

Although you may dream of a top of the range sewing machine, as a beginner that's really not necessary. Really, to start with all you need is a basic straight stitch! If you find you enjoy sewing though, you'll quickly out-grow an entry-level machine – especially if you wish to work on larger quilting projects. So, there are a few pointers opposite for when you upgrade.

Many of the smaller, compact machines are programmed with lots of stitches and come with several feet. However, if you have the budget, there are machines that are particularly suited to quilting: look for a large throat and extension table. Some manufacturers make tables that your machine sits in to help support larger projects. A built-in walking foot is useful, as is the ability to drop the feed dogs from the front of the machine, without taking off the extension table.

Looks are important, but check out all the features of that pretty machine before you buy! Some machines like this one will sew without a foot pedal – they use a stop/start button and speed control on the machine.

My sewing machine.

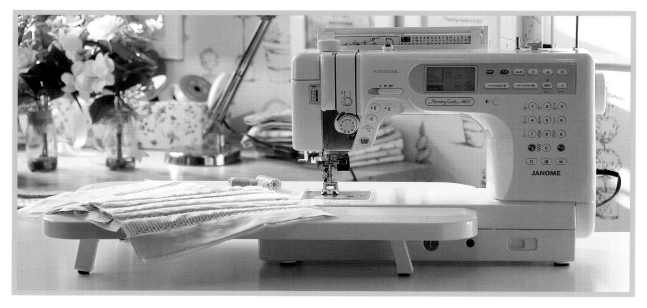

12

WHAT TO LOOK FOR

⊕ Look for a computerized sewing machine; you'll find a wide range stitches for both utility and decorative effects, and the digital interface makes them easier to select.

⊕ A needle threader is a must-have! It makes threading so much quicker, particularly when you're changing the colour of your thread regularly.

⊕ A needle up/down function allows you to start and stop sewing with the needle up or down in your work. This is handy when pivoting or stop/starting free-motion embroidery (see page 44). It also means the needle is in the correct 'up' position when you remove your work, freeing the thread from the tension discs and allowing it to pull through freely.

⊕ A drop feed dog facility is helpful for free-motion embroidery (see also page 44), some machines come with a plate that covers the feed dogs to make them inactive.

⊕ Some machines will come with a knee lift that enables you to lift the presser foot with your knee, leaving your hands free to continue sewing your work. This feature is useful when you're stippling your quilt or machine appliquéing curved designs.

⊕ The pressure foot pressure can be adjusted on some machines, and this is a useful feature for quilting in particular – your quilt sandwich will need less pressure than when sewing just fabric, due to its thickness.

⊕ A speed control may be useful to new sewers. These machines usually work without the foot pedal, using a 'start/stop' button on the front of the machine.

⊕ If you are taking your quilting to the next level, domestic longarm sewing machines are also available (see below). These have an extra-large throat (which is the area to the right of the needle), allowing bulky quilts to be manoeuvred more easily. These machines also come with a large bed or table that can take a greater bulk of fabric.

Most dealers will allow you to 'test-drive' a sewing machine before you buy and so are well worth a visit – it is always worth taking your time choosing, as a sewing machine could last you a lifetime if well looked after. Alternatively, visit one of the many sewing exhibitions where you'll find a range of manufacturers displaying their machines. Again, you'll be able to try them out and perhaps purchase at a favourable price!

Sewing machine accessories. These almost always come with a newly purchased machine.

For those who do a lot of quilting, you may wish to invest in a longarm machine – these machines have space to hold larger quilts and are often programmed with lots of stitch designs. If these machines are out of your budget, many quilt stores offer a quilting service.

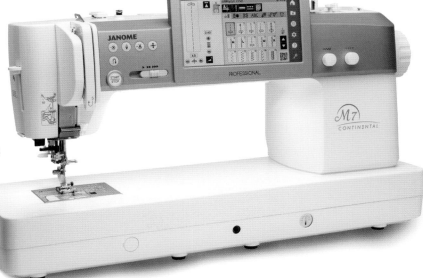

MACHINE FEET

There are many presser feet available for your sewing machine, each with a unique job to do, making sewing techniques easier and your finished work look professional. Most domestic sewing-machine feet will clip onto an adaptor or 'ankle' on the end of the take-up lever; some you will need to screw on. Below are the feet I use the most for quilting projects. Presser feet may vary in appearance from one manufacturer to another – always buy the recommended feet for your machine.

Standard/zigzag foot

This foot will be fitted to your machine when you first take it out of the box. It will have a wide hole for the needle to pass through and enable it to 'swing' from side to side when using zigzag or decorative stitches without the needle hitting the foot. This is the foot you'll use for most of your projects.

Quarter-inch foot

This foot is used only with a straight stitch. It gives you a perfect ¼in (5mm) seam allowance; simply guide your fabric along the side of your foot and the needle will be exactly ¼in (5mm) away from the edge.

Walking foot

This is one of the feet you'll need to screw on. Take off the 'ankle' by unscrewing it (make sure you put it somewhere safe!) then attach the walking foot to the side of the take-up lever, making sure the bar at the side sits on top of the needle clamp. The motion of the needle going up and down activates the grippers on the bottom of the foot, feeding the fabric through evenly from both the top and bottom. This makes the foot a must-have for quilters, as you will be working with multiple layers of fabric and wadding/batting. A walking foot is also useful for sewing together different weights of fabric, such as curtains with lining, or slippery fabrics like velvet and satin. Don't be concerned about the noise: the mechanism inside the foot can make your machine sound louder than usual!

Satin stitch/appliqué foot

This foot has two ski-like panels on the bottom, to raise the foot over satin stitches which are usually quite three-dimensional as the needle takes the thread over the same spot a few times. These feet are usually transparent so you can see the exact position of the stitch.

Free-motion/darning foot

This is another foot that is usually screwed onto the take-up lever. As with the walking foot, there is a bar that sits over the needle clamp. This makes the foot 'hop' across your fabric as you sew. Most darning feet have an open section and some will be clear plastic.

Overedge foot

Use this foot with an overedge stitch to take the thread around the raw edge of your fabric. The foot has a blade-like prong that helps to tuck in stray threads.

Stitch in the ditch foot

This foot has a guide in the centre of the foot which is placed over the seam, to allow the quilting stitch to be guided precisely over the seam.

Seam guide

A seam guide fits into the ankle of your sewing machine, or into the back of your walking foot, and provides a guide to feed your fabric against for straight line sewing – this is perfect for cross-hatch quilting or pin tucking.

SEWING MACHINE NEEDLES

Needles are sized in metric and imperial. The smaller the number the finer the needle, and the size of a needle is calculated by its diameter; for example an 80 needle is 0.8mm in diameter. Understanding needles and their associated numbers will help you to make the correct choice for your fabric and thread, resulting in perfect seams. It really makes a difference to your work when you use the correct needle, and quilting needles are specifically engineered for use in both fabric piecing and quilting your work. They are designed with a slim shaft to enable them to pass through layers of fabric smoothly. Quilting needles are generally sized 80/12–90/14.

WHEN THINGS GO WRONG

Two tips to start with: re-threading your machine will solve most of your stitching problems, and always make sure you have a clean, lint-free machine. But, if those don't work…

⊕ Is your thread decent quality? Cheaper threads can be made from shorter fibres that can easily break.

⊕ Check the route of your thread. Occasionally it can become tangled in the threading system, particularly around the top of the take-up lever.

⊕ Check that the thread is coming off the spool smoothly. There are sometimes small nicks around the top of the spool that can catch the thread and eventually snap it.

⊕ If your thread is breaking at the needle, it may be too thick for the size of the needle, which will cause friction.

⊕ Change the needle for a new one. There may be a slight bend in the needle, or it may be blunt.

⊕ Re-thread the machine both top and bottom, just in case one of the threading stages has been missed.

⊕ Don't pull or push your fabric through the machine: that's the job of the feed dogs!

⊕ Check that your needle is pushed into the needle holder as far as it will go. After a few hours of sewing it may have worked loose and dropped down a little.

⊕ Is your needle fitted the right way round? Most domestic machines will take the flat part of the needle to the back of the holder.

⊕ If it looks like a bird's nest under your work, there's a problem with the top thread. Make sure the tension is engaged by taking the thread as far as the needle, then putting the presser foot down. It should be quite difficult to pull the thread through if it is passing through the tension discs correctly.

⊕ This is a bobbin tension problem (the small spool of thread under your needle plate). Take out the bobbin and re-thread, making sure the thread passes through the grooves in the side of the bobbin holder. Check the bobbin is sitting in the holder the right way round – refer to your user manual for help.

TOOLS & EQUIPMENT

SCISSORS

You'll need a few pairs of scissors that are wholly dedicated to fabrics, along with paper scissors to cut out pattern templates. Many fabric scissors are available for both left- and right-handed use, some with soft grip handles, some with a spring-action that helps to open the blades after each cut and reduce hand strain. A good pair of scissors can last you a lifetime so don't scrimp on price, and make sure you take care of them.

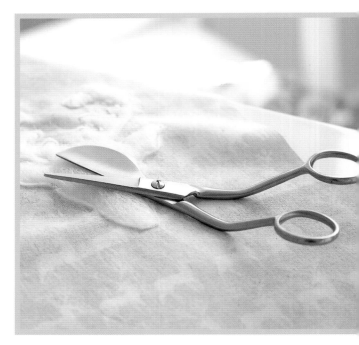

⊕ A pair of **dressmaking shears** of high quality will last you for years. Unlike regular scissors, shears have one handle larger than the other; the blades are also bent to allow the blade to sit as flat as possible on your cutting surface, allowing for maximum control as you're cutting. I tend to use shears with a 10in (25cm) blade. If the weight of the shears is an issue for you, look for plastic handles as they will be lighter than steel.

⊕ **Embroidery scissors** are handy for trimming threads and are essential for snipping into curves. Make sure they are sharp right to the point for accurate, neat cutting.

⊕ The blades on **pinking shears** make small zigzag cuts; the 45-degree angle of the cut helps to prevent woven fabrics from fraying, making it a quick way to finish seams. They are also useful for trimming seams around curves – an alternative way of 'snipping into curves'. Used on non-woven fabric such as felt, a decorative effect is created.

⊕ **Appliqué** (or **duckbilled**) **scissors** have one flat blade that sits under the fabric and prevents you from cutting through the seam. These are ideal for trimming appliqué shapes that you haven't quite sewn over the edge of the fabric!

16

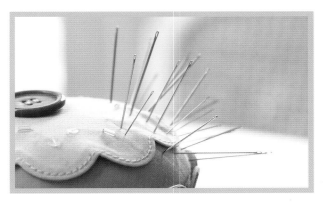

HAND-SEWING NEEDLES

⊕ Needles vary in length, point shape and thickness depending on their purpose. I'd suggest keeping a pack of sharps in various sizes in your sewing kit for general use.

⊕ Needles designed especially for hand quilting are called **betweens** (seen on page 82), and these are small, strong needles with a round eye. Their size and strength mean they can pass through multiple layers yet still create small stitches.

⊕ If you are big stitch quilting (see page 84) you will need a thicker thread and larger stitches, so use an **embroidery needle** as this has a larger eye and a sharp point.

⊕ With all needles, the larger the number of a needle, the smaller the size.

THIMBLES

⊕ A must-have for hand quilters! There are many different types of thimbles on the market – leather, rubber, plastic or metal. Try different types and see which you get on with. I like to use a leather thimble for hand quilting, but you may find a metal one easier – your choice!

TAPE MEASURE

⊕ Always buy a plastic tape measure, as fabric tape measures may stretch!

PINCUSHIONS

⊕ There are pincushions for the wrist, for your sewing machine, on the lids of jam jars and sewing boxes, patchworked, vintage, large, small and even novelty pincushions in the form of anything from hedgehogs to fruit. It's your choice! I like a pincushion that can accommodate my glass- and flower-head pins, machine- and hand-sewing needles and a few quilters' safety pins too. A sturdy base prevents it from rolling across my table, and I push my doll needles straight through the centre of the long body of the pincushion to protect them from breakage. Here's something you may not know: the little strawberry that is attached to many tomato-shaped pincushions is filled with sand to help keep your pins sharp!

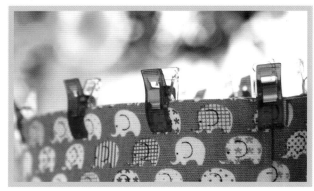

GLASS HEAD PINS

⊕ Pins need to be long and strong, and visible! They'll be holding your patchwork pieces together before sewing, keeping paper patterns against the fabric as you cut, and may even need to go through your quilt sandwich. Go for multicoloured glass heads – the colours will stand out against patterned fabric, and the glass heads do not melt if you catch them with an iron. Strong and rust-proof stainless steel shafts work best – as most of your quilting projects will be made from cotton, the fabric will take a thicker pin without leaving holes.

QUILTERS' SAFETY PINS

⊕ Use these to tack/baste your quilt sandwich together – the curve of the pins makes them easier to place in your quilt when it's lying flat.

FLOWER HEAD PINS

⊕ These are usually longer than glass head pins, but are quite fine so will bend easily. The plastic head is large and flat, and will stand out on your work and if dropped on the floor!

FABRIC CLIPS

⊕ These are a suitable alternative to pins, especially when working with heavy fabrics, thick layers of fabric or piping that can be difficult to pin. They come in numerous colours and sizes and some manufacturers will add seam allowance markings on the flat side. Remove the clips as you sew.

ROTARY CUTTER, RULER & MAT

I've grouped these three items as they go hand in hand. I use this method of cutting probably more than I use scissors, certainly for cutting quick, accurate straight lines.

⊕ A 45mm-blade rotary cutter is the most useful size and many rotary cutters can be adjusted for left- or right-handed cutting. Always cover the blade with a safety guard after every cut (this will soon become a habit), as these blades are incredibly sharp. It is easy to ruin a blade by accidentally cutting over a stray pin, so make sure your cutting mat is clear of anything metal. 28mm cutters are useful for cutting around curves or following acrylic templates and 60mm blades will make light work of multiple layers of fabric or larger projects. Always dispose of the blades safely – even a blade that you'd consider to be blunt can still be dangerous.

⊕ Choose a 24 x 6in (61 x 15cm) ruler with $\frac{1}{8}$in (3mm) increments. You'll find 30-degree, 45-degree and 60-degree markings, and these are useful for measuring on the bias or marking grids on your fabric for quilting. Some rulers are frosted so that the grid lines stand out against your fabric; some have markings in black and white for the same reason. The ruler you use with a rotary cutter should be at least $\frac{1}{8}$in (3mm) thick to help stop the blade from slipping over the ruler when cutting. There are many shapes and sizes of rulers and quilting templates available to buy, but for the beginner sewer this one ruler should suit most projects.

⊕ You'll need a mat to protect both your table and the blade of your rotary cutter – the larger the better! If you're taking a mat to a workshop you may wish to invest in two: a large one for your sewing room and a smaller, more portable size for classes. Some mats will be in inches on one side and centimetres on the other, with many diagonal markings for bias cutting and measuring angles. Try to store your mat flat when not in use to prevent it buckling, and keep it clean – I've spoiled a straight cut in the past by not removing a blob of glue which dried hard!

A self-healing cutting mat is a worthwhile investment – the cuts you make simply close over, prolonging the life of your mat. These mats tend to grip your fabric slightly, unlike hard plastic mats, and there's less chance of your blade slipping. These mats benefit from moisture, so cleaning with warm water occasionally is a good idea, and rotate the mat every now and again to avoid cutting on the same spot over and over again.

Rotary cutter, quilting ruler and mat.

IRON

⊕ An iron is an essential tool for a successful sewer. Many of us will wash our fabric before starting a project – besides possible shrinkage after a first wash, even fabric that comes straight off the bolt will be creased, so a steam iron is useful in these instances. However, when sewing your quilt pieces together don't use steam or move the iron around the fabric, as these can cause the seams to curve. Instead, press the seam to set the stitches by placing the iron over the seam without moving it. Then press again with the seam either open or to one side, depending on the pattern or your preference! If you have light and dark fabrics, press the seam over towards the darker fabric so that the seam doesn't show through the light side.

⊕ If you need to iron your finished quilt, use a cool setting and a pressing cloth. Steam could be used also, if you wish, depending on the fibre content of your wadding/batting.

SEAM RIPPER/QUICK UNPICK

⊕ Part of almost any sewing project involves unpicking, whether that's tacking/basting stitches or inevitable mistakes! Keep a few unpickers in your sewing box; they will eventually blunt, and when they do so it can become difficult to glide through unwanted stitches.

BAMBOO POINTER AND CREASER

⊕ A perfect little tool for creasing fabric, this is handy to have for projects which include quilt-as-you-go techniques for when your finger gets tired from finger pressing (not shown)!

EMBROIDERY HOOPS

⊕ Use a large embroidery hoop for small hand-quilting projects. Quilting hoops are available for larger designs; these are deeper than regular embroidery hoops, which makes them stronger and able to take the weight of fabric.

LAP AND FLOOR FRAMES

⊕ As an alternative to embroidery hoops, lap and floor frames can be used for hand quilting. Like the hoops, a lap frame is ideal for smaller, on-the-go designs; floor frames are perfect for larger quilts.

ADHESIVES

I keep a good selection of adhesives in my store cupboard: temporary and permanent, fabric and paper – they're all useful. If you're using any kind of adhesive with machine-sewn projects, make sure they are suitable for use with machines. You don't want to cause any damage to your sewing machine by getting glue inside it. Make sure your adhesives are designed for fabrics, so they will not stain and will wash out. (The permanent adhesive sprays won't wash away.)

⊕ **Repositionable spray fabric adhesive** is a quick alternative to tacking/basting fabric. I use it often to hold appliqué shapes in place while sewing; it's also excellent for keeping layers of fabric and wadding/batting from puckering under the machine, making it a quick and easy option for assembling your 'quilt sandwich'.

⊕ There are various types of **permanent adhesives**. A **permanent spray adhesive** is particularly useful for a quilted project, in particular applying appliqué – simply spray it onto the wrong side of your fabric before adding your appliqué then, once ironed, the piece is permanently adhered. A **glue pen** is invaluable for English paper piecing. Other wet tacking/basting glues are a good alternative to pins for attaching trimmings and inserting a zip.

⊕ **Fusible adhesive sheets** are placed between fabrics then ironed to fuse the two layers in place permanently. Paper-backed adhesive sheets are particularly useful – you can draw onto the paper backing before cutting out your shapes, using patterns, templates or simply drawing free hand. Bear in mind that, as you're drawing on the back of the fabric, letters and numbers will need to be reversed. The paper side is then removed, stuck to the fabric, placed onto the main fabric surface with adhesive side down, then the three layers ironed to keep all in position. They are ideal for appliqué, and are a great way to prevent fraying and puckering – in some cases, you may not even need to sew!

SPRAY STARCH

⊕ I use starch particularly with patchwork. It gives my fabric a crispness and makes it easy to finger press. I find it also helps when bag making, if I need to stiffen my fabric a little.

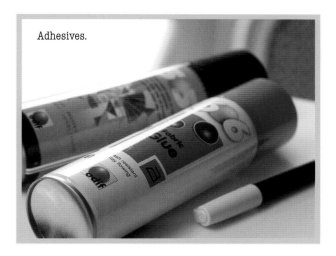
Adhesives.

Fusible sheets.

MARKING TOOLS

Whether you're free-hand drawing or using templates and rulers, you will probably have to mark your fabric at some point, and there are lots of products to choose from!

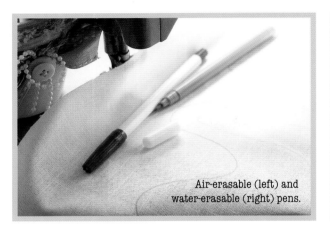

Air-erasable (left) and water-erasable (right) pens.

Heat-erasable pens.

Chalk.

Quilt pounce.

⊕ **Air-erasable pens** use ink that disappears after around 24 hours. Don't use these on a project that takes a few days to complete! Be careful not to iron over your markings, as the ink becomes permanent!

⊕ **Water-erasable pens** use ink that is removed with a damp cloth or washing. Like the air-erasable pens, make sure you don't iron over the ink to avoid setting it permanently.

⊕ **Chalk** is available in block or pen form and comes in many colours. Its benefit is that it brushes away easily, but this is not ideal for hand sewing – as the fabric passes through your hands, the chalk lines can disappear.

⊕ **Heat-erasable pens** use an ink that disappears when ironed or rubbed. Always test these pens on a spare piece of the fabric you're using, as sometimes they can bleach the fabric. This is not a problem if you're marking within the seam allowance, but you need to be careful with these if you're marking quilting lines on your fabric. Avoid using heat-erasable pens when hand quilting; the heat from your hands can make the lines disappear as you sew – I learned this from experience!

⊕ **Quilt pounces** are chalk-filled pads that are used with stencils. Different colours of chalk are available to help your design stand out no matter what colour fabric you're using.

QUILTING TEMPLATES

Marking your quilting design with templates is an easy and effective way of achieving perfectly quilted patterns. There are hundreds to choose from! Remember, you will need to mark your quilt top after you create your quilt sandwich (see page 42).

(see page 42)

This feather design can either be used as a border, or to completely cover your quilt!

- **Acrylic templates** that work with specially designed presser feet are available, and they allow you to sew your pattern around the templates without the need for marking. The presser feet look like your free-motion/darning feet but without the spring, so they don't 'hop' as your regular free-motion feet would. Follow the manufacturer's instructions; many have video tutorials which will help you to get the most out of the templates.

- With **plastic templates** you'll need to mark your fabric, on smaller pieces you can use air- or water-erasable ink pens, chalk pens or fabric pencils. Use your free-motion/darning foot on your sewing machine, and simply sew over the lines!

- On larger projects you'll find it quicker to use a **quilt pounce.** Place the template over the fabric and sweep the pad across the top. Move the template to the next position, matching the pattern, and repeat.

- **Paper patterns** will need to be traced either directly onto your fabric, or onto quilters' paper, which can then be torn away after sewing. If you have a large project or intend to use these patterns frequently, it may be worth investing in a light box. Simply place the pattern on the box, your fabric right side up on top, and use any of your marking tools to trace the design. If a light box isn't an option, tape the pattern to a window on a sunny day; alternatively, a glass-topped table with a lamp underneath works a treat!

QUILTING FABRICS

Generally, 100 per cent cotton works best for quilts. It handles beautifully, holds its shape, creases well, is breathable, hard-wearing and available in an endless choice of colours and prints. A quilting cotton has a slightly loose weave which makes it easy to hand-sew; linen is a good option for the same reason.

To pre-wash or not? Have a think about usage. If your project will be laundered then it's worth pre-washing the fabric. This way you can make sure any shrinkage or colour running happens before you start sewing. Use the washing instructions on the bolt or, if you're not sure, wash on a cool cycle. Press pre-washed fabric whilst damp before you start to sew. In the case of bags which are unlikely to go in the wash, I don't normally pre-wash. You can always treat the finished article with a spray fabric protector if you wish. For those who prefer a vintage look to their quilts, don't pre-wash (but still test your fabric for colour-fastness first) then wash your quilt when it's finished. It will shrink slightly and give a crinkled effect.

PRE-CUT FABRIC

Pre-cut bundled fabric is an excellent choice for both new and experienced quilters. If you add up the yardage, packs of pre-cut fabrics can work out to be more expensive than buying by the yard, but – especially for the newbie – you know that the colours and prints of the fabric have been put together to match perfectly, so that you can just dip into the bundle and piece fabrics together and they'll match (see also page 26). For more advanced sewers, it gives you an opportunity to buy small pieces of co-ordinating fabrics that may not be available off the bolt. I don't think my local fabric store would be too pleased if I asked for a 2½in (6.5cm) strip of my chosen fabric to be cut from the bolt! Opposite are the most popular sizes:

Fat quarter

A yard (metre) of fabric cut into four squares usually measuring 18 x 22in (46 x 56cm). (See below.)

Squares

Packs of square pieces of fabric come in sizes from 1in (2.5cm) to 10in (25cm) and everything in between! These pre-cut squares of perfectly blended colours save you the job of cutting, so you can get on with the enjoyable bit – the sewing! You will typically find these in packs of anything from twenty-four to fifty pieces.

Strips

Sometimes rolled up together (see right), strips of co-ordinating fabrics usually measure 44 x 2½in (112 x 6.5cm). They are useful for patchworkers who will either sew together the strips or cut them into shapes to be joined back together again to create patterns. The number of strips in each pack varies from around twenty to forty.

Fat quarters (top) and squares and strips (above).

UNDERSTANDING FAT QUARTERS AND EIGHTHS

A yard of fabric from the bolt will most commonly measure 44 x 36in (112 x 92cm). Cut this in half widthways and lengthways and you'll have four equal pieces measuring 22 x 18in (56 x 46cm). These are fat quarters.

Cut in half again and, depending on which way you cut, these pieces will measure either 11 x 18in (28 x 46cm) or 22 x 9in (56 x 23cm). These are fat eighths.

Fat sixteenths aren't so common, but are half the fat eighth, measuring 11x 9in (28 x 23cm).

A strip measuring 44 x 9in (112 x 23cm) is known as a long quarter.

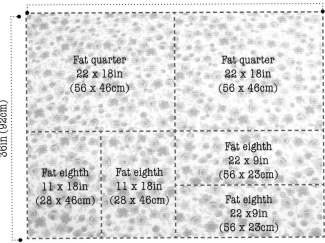

44in (112cm)

36in (92cm)

Fat quarter
22 x 18in
(56 x 46cm)

Fat quarter
22 x 18in
(56 x 46cm)

Fat eighth
11 x 18in
(28 x 46cm)

Fat eighth
11 x 18in
(28 x 46cm)

Fat eighth
22 x 9in
(56 x 23cm)

Fat eighth
22 x9in
(56 x 23cm)

A yard (metre) of fabric.

BACKING FABRIC

The most popular backing fabric for your quilt is plain or patterned cotton. If you're making a large item, extra wide quilting fabric is available, although you may prefer to use sheeting fabric, which is sometimes folded on the roll, making it up to 108in (275cm) wide. It may be more affordable to use an actual bed sheet, but make sure it's a few inches bigger than the fabric you're quilting. If it's for a toddler quilt, try flannel or fleece for the backing to make it snuggly and soft. Calico is a good alternative backing for wall hangings and home décor items.

CHOOSING YOUR QUILT COLOURS

Mixing colours and patterns of fabric can be the most confusing aspect of making a quilt! This is where pre-cuts come into their own. You'll have in mind your own specific colour choices, plain or patterned. If you're purely quilting the fabric, anything goes. However, if you're patchworking before quilting, there are a few things to bear in mind. How big are your patchwork sizes? You don't want to lose the pattern when the fabric is cut into small pieces. Do your colours have very dark and light values? In which case, you'll need to be careful how you place them: the eye will be drawn to an odd dark fabric mixed in with light, which could spoil the effect of your design.

If you want an area of the design to stand out, surround it with a plain fabric to give it space. Solids, or tone-on-tone fabrics allow the patterns to take centre stage. And don't forget, you may want to use one of your fabrics as the border and another for the binding, so make sure you purchase enough before you start!

Colour choice is subjective, so the main thing is to choose the colours you like and will enjoy working with.

FABRIC TERMINOLOGY

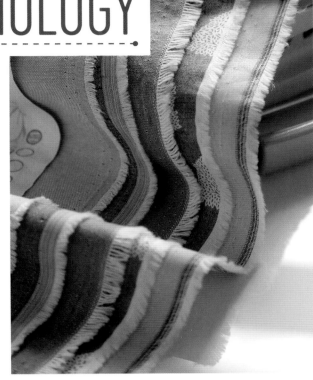

RIGHT/WRONG SIDES

The right side of your fabric is the side you want to see. This is quite clear on a printed fabric as the right side will be brighter than the wrong side. With some fabrics, it can be difficult to determine which is right and wrong as the two look very similar. A rule of thumb is to look at the little holes in the selvedge/selvage. These holes are made by small hooks that hold the fabric on rollers as it goes through various processes; they push through the fabric from the back to the front, making the holes on the right side slightly raised. Run your finger over them: the rougher side will be the right side. If this doesn't work and you really can't tell the difference, then the chances are that nobody else will. Just make sure you use the same side for each part of your project, so mark one side with either quilters' safety pins or chalk.

ROLL

Furnishing and dressmaking fabric usually comes on a roll, with the fabric information on a swing tag. The width of fabric varies; some may be folded in half. You may find it useful to take a picture of the tag, particularly if it has washing instructions or in case you need to buy more of the same fabric.

SELVEDGE/SELVAGE

The selvedges are the edges on either side of the fabric as it comes off the roll – tightly woven strips that prevent the fabric from unravelling or fraying. Sometimes they are printed with the name of the manufacturer, sometimes there will be coloured dots that refer to the colours of the print. Although you don't use the selvedges as they are usually a tighter weave than the fabric and may have small holes in them, it's a good idea to save a small piece in case you need to colour match your fabrics. Cut off the selvedges before you start your sewing projects but don't throw them away. Some selvedges are quite pretty and can be used as trimmings.

WARP AND WEFT

This is the same as the grain (see right): the warp is lengthways and the weft is widthways (think 'weft to right'...).

BOLT

A bolt is simply the cardboard block that fabric is wound around. Most commonly this will be quilting or craft cotton, folded in half (wrong sides together). Take a look at the end of the bolt before you buy – there is important information there regarding the fabric content, manufacturer, width of fabric and price.

GRAIN

This describes the direction of woven threads. The lengthways grain is parallel to the selvedge/selvage (see left), running the length of the fabric. The crosswise grain runs from side to side (selvedge to selvedge). The bias grain is at a 45-degree angle diagonally across the fabric. Cutting your fabric on the grain ensures you achieve the best drape for dressmaking and curtains, but for smaller crafty projects this isn't so important. Curtains not cut on the grain tend to twist. I found this with some shop-bought curtains, and no amount of pressing would make them hang straight.

The bias grain has the most stretch, making it perfect for binding and piping. Skirt and dress patterns sometimes require the fabric to be cut on the bias to add a little 'give' to the garment.

WADDING

Choosing wadding/batting can be a bit of a minefield, so let's keep it simple. Wadding/batting is the padded layer that goes between the outer and lining fabrics of quilts, but I also use it in bag making, table runners, tea cosies and any project that needs a touch of luxury or added drape.

Read the manufacturer's instructions regarding pre-washing, shrinkage and quilting distance. Terms you may see are 'loft', which is the thickness of the wadding, and 'scrim', which is the polyester layer that holds some natural waddings together.

For quilting I like to use natural wadding/batting as it is breathable and soft. I always pre-wash the wadding/batting before making up my quilt sandwich. I prefer fusible fleece or foam stabilizer for bag making, but here's a brief description of the most popular waddings/battings.

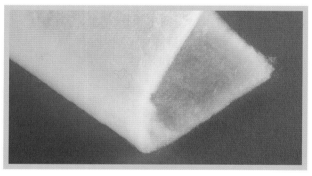

⊕ Synthetic **polyester** wadding/batting tends to have a high loft so is thicker than the natural alternative. Nowadays you can even find synthetic wadding/batting made from recycled plastic bottles!

⊕ **Natural** wadding/batting is made from cotton, wool, silk bamboo or soya, all usually softer and more breathable than synthetic. Cotton is ideal for quilts because of its high thermal value.

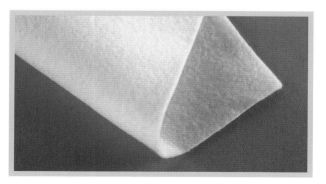

⊕ **Polyester-cotton** wadding/batting is usually eighty per cent cotton and twenty per cent polyester, forming a high-loft layer with the benefits of both materials, making it stable, warm but not weighty, and usually washable.

⊕ **Wool** wadding/batting is breathable, thermal and easily retains its loft, but may not be suitable for projects intended for regular use as it usually needs to be hand washed and dried flat.

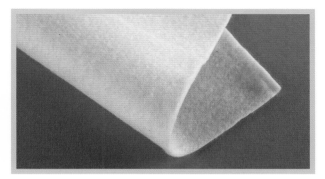

⊕ **Bamboo, silk and cotton** can be blended together to form a warm, luxurious wadding/batting which is particularly strong.

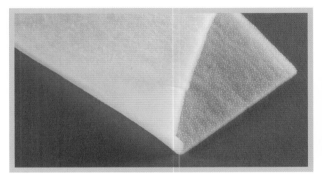

⊕ Choose a **fusible fleece** that is ironed onto the back of your fabric to give it form and stability. If you can't find fusible, use a sew-in wadding/batting and try a spray of repositionable adhesive to hold it in place while sewing.

⊕ Also available on the market is an insulated, **thermal** wadding/batting, which I use for oven gloves, tea cosies and mug hugs, to help keep my cuppa warm.

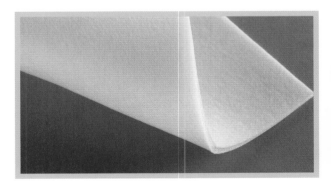

⊕ The new kid on the block is **foam stabilizer**, available to either fuse or sew in, which adds a real firmness to your project while remaining easy to sew through. Perfect if you want the item to stand up alone and keep its shape, you may need to trim it back to the seams to reduce bulk.

⊕ The term **'needle-punched'** simply means that the wadding/batting has been felted, by punching barbed needles through the material to help keep it stable.

THREADS

I always recommend a decent-quality thread, but what makes thread good quality? It's mainly the strength, called 'tensile' strength, which helps to lengthen the life of your seams. Avoid 'fluffy' threads and ensure the one you buy is smooth – as your thread will be travelling through the eye of your needle at high speed, an uneven thread can affect its strength and may even twist. In extreme cases, it could even wear out your tension discs. Inexpensive thread could also have rough filaments that build up inside your sewing machine.

It is recommended that you try to use the same fibre content as your fabric – cotton with cotton, polyester with synthetic, etc. – although I don't always follow the rules. There are also different weights of threads to consider. Here are the basics:

⊕ A 100 per cent cotton thread is the type of machine thread most used and favoured by quilters, as it is a natural fibre and withstands heat – important when pressing cotton fabrics. A quality cotton thread is made from the longer strands of cotton to strengthen your seams and is healthier for your sewing machine! I like to use cotton thread by Aurifil.

⊕ Top-stitching thread is a thick, strong polyester thread used for stitching that can be seen on top of your work (for example, on jeans).

⊕ Embroidery thread/floss is usually made from rayon as it's reflective and fine, designed to really show off your decorative stitches. I like to use this for hand quilting, especially for big stitch quilting (see page 84).

⊕ Hand-quilting thread is quite heavy and is coated to enable the thread to travel through your quilt sandwich easily. Alternatively, try waxing your thread using a beeswax block.

⊕ Specific bobbin thread for quilting is also available: The Bottom Line is a fine filament polyester thread that has been developed to sink into backing fabric leaving not much trace of colour. It also works well with stitch in the ditch and appliqué techniques.

⊕ Thread weights can be confusing but, put simply, a smaller weight number (wt) depicts a heavier thread. As a rough guide, choose a 40wt for quilting, 50wt or 60wt for appliqué and free-motion embroidery, and filling your bobbin. 20–30wt is a thick thread for top-stitching and decorative work. If your thread weight looks like a fraction – for example, 60/2 – the first number is the weight and the second is how many strands in the thread. If you're still confused then choose an all-purpose 50wt which should work with most of your projects.

⊕ With all your threads, invest in as many colours as you can so that you never have to compromise! A neutral grey or beige colour is a good choice for piecing fabrics as it will blend with most colours without 'shadowing' under the seam. If you're using a lot of white pieces then use white thread, and for quilting, any colour you like! Variegated threads can create a pretty effect; contrasting coloured thread will make your quilting stand out, or choose the same colour thread as your fabric to just create texture.

100 per cent cotton machine quilting thread.

Hand-quilting thread.

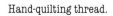

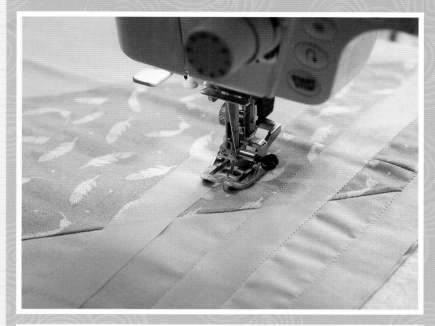

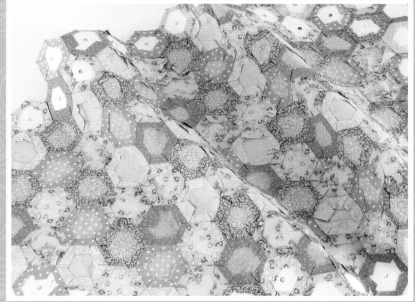

QUILTING
KNOW-HOW

CARING FOR YOUR QUILT

Having spent hours of your precious time making your quilt, once it's finished it is important that you look after and preserve it for everyone to enjoy – after all, it could become a family heirloom! A hand-made quilt (whether stitched on a machine or by hand) is a real treasure and should last a lifetime with proper care.

⊕ Quilts are made to be used and seen, but whether it's a bed quilt, a wall hanging or a snuggle quilt left on the sofa, **don't expose it to direct sunlight**. This will cause fading.

⊕ If you have to store your quilts, try not to fold them and instead **roll them up**, preferably around a tube, to avoid permanent creasing. Don't store your quilts in plastic bags either as this will cause them to discolour. For bed quilts or other large quilts, it's far better to lay them over a spare bed; if necessary, pile them up on top of each other.

⊕ When it comes to **washing your quilts**, for the odd mark a spot clean is fine. However, it is possible to machine wash a large quilt on a gentle programme, but make sure you avoid strong detergents. After a short, slow spin, dry the quilt flat or roll up in towels. When almost dry, a short tumble dry on a low heat will finish off the drying process and help fluff up the quilt.

Smaller quilted items, such as bags and pillow covers, are best spot cleaned or lightly sponged with a mild detergent, then left to dry naturally.

CUTTING

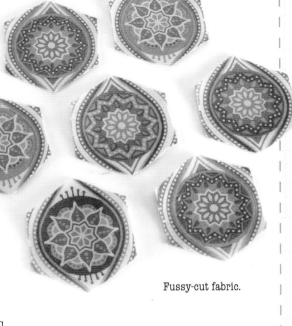

HOW TO GET THE BEST CUT

Cutting is an important part of sewing: the better your cutting, the better your sewing. If you are using shears, hold them firmly and upright when cutting, to achieve the best cut. Metal handles help when cutting through thick fabrics, but can be a little tiring on the hand. Plastic and comfort handled shears are also available. Shears come in many different sizes. Try an 8–9in (20–23cm) blade if you're a beginner, or larger if you're more experienced at cutting and want to cut quickly or through thick fabrics.

When using a rotary cutter, for safety only have the blade exposed when cutting. They are extremely sharp! Place your hand on your ruler with your fingers away from the edge, and keep the blade at right angles to your work. Tacky sprays are available to help hold quilting rulers in place as you work.

Fussy-cut fabric.

FUSSY CUTTING

This is a method of cutting a specific area of your fabric to centralize a pattern, which you can see top right. Place a transparent ruler or template over the pattern you wish to cut out. Mark around the area with an erasable pen, then cut. You may want to use a specific part of a print for a central design on your quilt, or on a flap or pocket on a bag, when having half the print just wouldn't look right!

CUTTING ACROSS CORNERS

This helps to keep the corners square when turned the right way out. Cut away the corner, keeping as close to the stitches as you can without snipping them.

TRIMMING CURVES

For curves that are to be turned, make little 'v'-shaped cuts into the fabric up to the seam – this will stop the fabric from puckering when turned the right way out. You could also use pinking shears for the same effect.

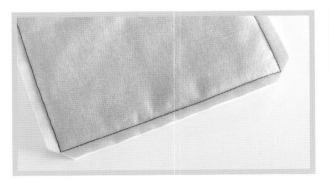

MACHINE STITCHES

You may have two or two hundred stitches on your machine – utility stitches for project construction and decorative stitches for embellishment. Take a look in the manufacturer's manual to see the recommended presser feet to use with the different stitches. In most cases the feet are lettered and some machines will display the foot required on the screen. These are the stitches I use the most.

Top to bottom: straight line quilting in the ditch, straight line outline quilting and top-stitching.

STRAIGHT STITCH

The most useful stitch on your machine! Use for joining fabric, gathering, top-stitching and tacking/basting. You should be able to alter the length of the stitch where necessary on your machine. On many machines, the stitch width function will swing the needle from left to right. By contrast, adjusting the length of the stitch doesn't affect the needle: it changes the rate at which the feed dogs draw the fabric through. A shorter stitch forms a strong seam and is preferable to use with fine fabrics. The majority of sewing machines will default to a 2.4 or 2.5mm stitch length – this is suitable for most fabrics. Long stitches are sewn with a looser tension and are easy to remove, making them an appropriate choice for tacking/basting. You may prefer the look of a longer stitch when top-stitching your project.

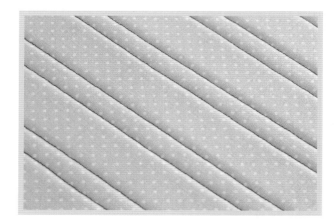

STRAIGHT LINE QUILTING

Straight line quilting in the ditch (see also page 60) is a popular technique, particularly with beginners. However, if the stitches waver, it can spoil the effect. Stitching ¼in (5mm) on each side of the seam gives a neat finish and is easier for a beginner quilter. This is known as outline or echo quilting (see page 74).

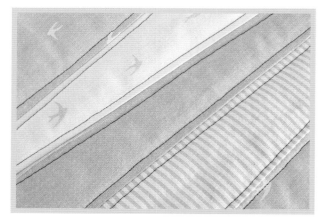

TOP-STITCHING

This is a straight stitch that is deliberately visible and seen from the front of your project. An edge-stitch is a straight stitch sewn close to the edge of your work.

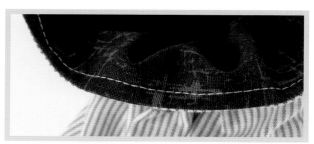

34

ZIGZAG STITCH

Neatening seams, appliqué, sewing on buttons, darning, free-motion embroidery and decorative trims make the zigzag stitch a must-have on your sewing machine. The width can be altered – when the length of the stitch is shortened it forms a bold line, called a 'satin' stitch, which is used for appliqué.

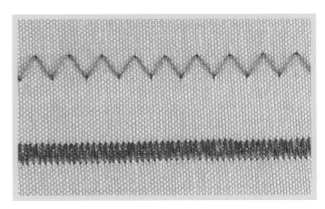

Top to bottom:
regular zigzag stitch, satin stitch.

BLIND HEM STITCH

This stitch sews along the inside of your hem with a straight stitch, then occasionally throws a zigzag stitch into the fold of the hem, catching just a couple of threads to keep the stitches as invisible as possible from the right side of your project. Used mostly for dressmaking and curtains, this is also a useful stitch for adding appliqué. A blind hem stitch foot, which has an adjustable guide, makes this stitch easier to sew but you can still select and sew the stitch on your machine without it – you just need to go slowly.

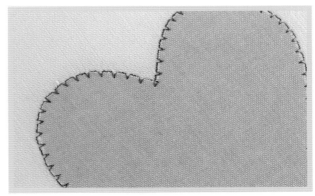

OVEREDGE STITCH

This stitch works best with an overedge foot (see page 14). The thread wraps around the edge of the fabric, finishing off seams and helping to prevent fraying. A great alternative to an overlocker/serger if you're not ready for that investment yet…

DECORATIVE STITCHES

Decorative stitches add interest to your project, although if you're quilting a bed-sized quilt you'll find them quite time consuming! Many machines come equipped with a wide choice of stitches that can be sewn over or alongside the seams. Try using embroidery thread/floss in contrasting colours to add a fun element; alternatively, a white thread on white fabric can look really elegant.

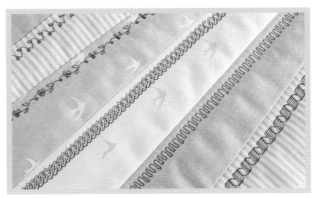

MOCK HAND STITCH

This is a clever stitch that uses clear thread on the top of the machine and coloured thread on the bottom. Increase the tension on the top of your machine to its maximum and the bottom thread will be pulled through to the top. The result is a row of alternating clear and coloured thread, giving the illusion of a hand-sewn running stitch! Perfect for quilters or to add a hand-made touch to bags, pockets, collars or even bed linen.

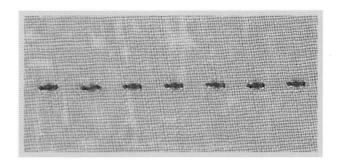

HAND STITCHES

Although much of your work will use the sewing machine, there are a few hand stitches you'll find useful for invisibly sewing openings closed, or tacking/basting zips, for example.

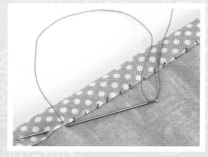

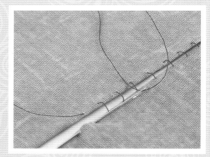

Tacking/basting stitch
A long running stitch used to temporarily hold fabrics together while sewing; the stitches are removed after the project is finished. I find it easier to tack/baste a zip in place rather than use pins, which can be difficult to sew around.

Slip stitch
Use this stitch along the fold of bias tape to secure. Take the needle into the base fabric, bring it up through the fold of the tape, then back directly underneath and repeat. I've used a contrasting colour of thread here so that you can see the stitch, but use the same colour as the binding for the most impressive results.

Ladder stitch
Used for bringing together two folded lengths of fabric, for instance when closing an opening in the lining of a bag, or closing a seam in a stuffed toy. Sew into the fold on one side with a small stitch, take the needle straight across the gap and into the opposite fold, sew into the fold again and repeat. After sewing a few stitches, gently pull the thread and the gap will close. Use the same colour thread as your fabric or, for the most invisible stitches on patterned fabric, choose a grey or beige thread.

Blanket stitch
One of my favourite stitches, a blanket stitch can be used to edge your fabric or add appliqué. Try to keep the stitches evenly spaced but don't worry if they are slightly uneven – this just adds to the hand-made look! I try to keep my stitches ¼in (5mm) apart; a couple of marks on your thumb can help with spacing.

APPLIQUÉ

Appliqué is the method of applying a decorative fabric shape to your project. This could be anything, from hearts or flowers to animals or sport-themed motifs – the list goes on!

⊕ There are many stitches you can use to decorate and secure your appliqué shape to your quilt, that you can either sew by hand or by machine. My favourite is blanket stitch, which I like to sew by hand (see opposite page and example on page 38); however, my sewing machine has this stitch too, along with other decorative stitches (see page 31). For example, satin stitch works well on the edge of appliqué.

⊕ The easiest way to adhere the appliqué shape is to use fusible webbing (see below) – sheets of paper-backed adhesive web that can be fused to the shape and permanently stick it to your background fabric before sewing. It also helps to stop the appliqué fraying. An alternative to fusible webbing is repositionable spray fabric adhesive. I'd avoid pinning, particularly on smaller shapes, as it can be difficult to manoeuvre and sew around the pins.

⊕ If you are machine sewing the edges of your appliqué, I recommend that you use a satin stitch/appliqué foot on your machine (see page 14). They are clear, so you can see the exact position of the stitch.

⊕ Use a top thread that either matches or co-ordinates with your appliqué fabric. The bobbin thread should be the same colour as your background fabric.

⊕ If you're using an appliqué shape with a few parts, be aware of colour – try to avoid placing a very light appliqué fabric over very dark background fabric, as the darker colour may show through.

APPLYING APPLIQUÉ WITH FUSIBLE WEBBING

1 Draw your design on the paper side of the webbing – bear in mind the image will be reversed.

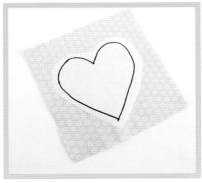

2 Roughly cut out the shape and place it over the wrong side of your fabric. When you are happy with the position, place a hot iron over the paper for a few seconds until the glue has set.

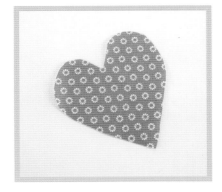

3 Cut out your appliqué shape. Peel away the paper backing – you may find scratching the back of the paper an easy way of removing it. Place the shape over your project and, again, iron in place.

APPLIQUÉ STITCH INSPIRATION

Time to choose your stitch! Tear-away stabilizer on the wrong side of the fabric will help to stop your appliqué puckering as you sew.

Machine stitches

Ensure you practise on a scrap piece of fabric first, as you may need to adjust the length and width of your stitch.

A **satin stitch** is a short zigzag stitch that creates a solid outline. Adjust the width, depending on the size of your appliqué. If you need a denser line, just sew over the outline twice.

Machine blanket stitch gives a great hand-made look to your work! Again, try adjusting the length and width of the stitch on a scrap piece of fabric until you're happy with it.

Free-motion embroidery has a sketchy, modern style. Embroider around the shape a few times and don't worry about the lines being perfectly straight – this adds to the look!

Use **blind hem stitch** if you don't want your stitches to stand out – the majority of the stitches will be just off the edge of the appliqué, with a small 'V' stitch occasionally catching the fabric.

Hand stitches

Try hand-sewing a **blanket stitch with embroidery thread/floss** for a folksy look.

Hand-sewn **running stitch** adds a great hand-made look to your work. Don't worry about the stitches all being the same length: variety adds to the rustic appearance.

If you prefer to hand-sew but don't want your stitching to show, **needle-turn appliqué** may be an option for you – I've deliberately used a contrasting thread colour so that you can see the stitches. Cut your fabric shapes approx. ⅛in (3mm) larger than required and pin, glue or hold the centre in position on the background fabric. Turn under the seam allowance of your appliqué with the aid of your needle, finger press and then sew in place with small ladder stitches. Repeat all around the shape. This technique gives more dimension to your work as the appliqué stands out from the background. However, it does take a lot longer to sew!

REVERSE APPLIQUÉ

Whereas appliqué is a method of applying shapes over the top of your work, reverse appliqué comes from behind, exposed through a cut-out hole in the shape you require. There are a few ways of doing this and here are two: one results in a neat edge and one with a raw edge.

Neat edge

You will need your top fabric, backing fabric and contrast fabric.

1 Draw the shape you require onto a piece of backing fabric, either on a piece of the same fabric you are using or sew-in interfacing. This section of fabric won't be seen, but choose a light-weight fabric so as not to add bulk to your project. Place the backing fabric over the top fabric, right sides together, positioning it where the hole is to be cut. Pin, then sew around the shape with a small stitch.

2 Remove the pins, cut out the hole in the centre, leaving a seam allowance of about ⅛in (3mm). Snip into any curves or corners.

3 Push the backing fabric through the hole and press.

4 Place contrasting fabric behind the hole and sew either by hand or machine. I've used a triple straight stitch.

Raw edge

You will need your top fabric and contrast fabric.

1 Draw the shape you require on the right side of your top fabric.

2 Cut a piece of contrast fabric slightly larger than your design, then lay your contrast fabric over the back of the top fabric. Pop a few pins through the outline of the design as a guide to help position the contrast fabric.

3 Sew around the design. This could be by hand, a straight stitch or free-motion stitching. Cut out the centre of the design leaving a seam allowance of about ⅛in (3mm).

QUILT SANDWICH

This is a term you'll hear a lot in the world of quilting. A quilt sandwich is simply made up of a quilt backing, a quilt top and a layer of wadding/batting in between the two.

If you're making a large quilt, the wadding/batting and backing should be 3–4in (7.75–10cm) larger than your quilt top. This allows for any 'shrinkage' or fabric shift when quilting. Smaller projects, or quilt-as-you-go techniques won't need such a large border.

To make the sandwich, press the backing fabric then place right side facing down. The reason you press the backing fabric is to make sure it is flat and smooth – it may help to tape the fabric to a flat surface with masking tape to keep it crease-free as you add the other layers.

Your wadding/batting should be around the same size as the backing fabric. Place this on top, patting out any wrinkles.

Your quilt top then goes centrally on top of the wadding/batting, right side up. It is worth checking at this point that there are no tails of thread on the back of your quilt top – these may show through or create little lumps on the right side of the fabric.

From right to left:
backing fabric, wadding/batting,
quilt top.

TACKING/BASTING YOUR QUILT SANDWICH

Tacking/basting your quilt will stop the layers shifting as you sew, so it's worth taking the time to make sure they are secure, flat and wrinkle free. There are several ways to hold your quilt sandwich together before quilting, so choose whichever works best for you.

⊕ **Pins.** Curved safety pins are ideal for tacking/basting your quilt sandwich. Your quilt sandwich should ideally be on a flat surface, and then the safety pins can scoop up the three layers in one go. Start either on one side or in the centre, and pin every 3–4in (7.75–10cm) or a hand-width apart. It's a good idea to avoid pinning over the lines you'll be sewing if possible, so that the pins can remain in place while quilting. Try to pin in a grid so the pins can be easily spotted for removal after quilting! You can also buy a special tool which will help you to close the quilters' safety pins, which avoids bunching up the quilt sandwich and prevents sore fingers!

⊕ **Spray tacking/basting.** Using a repositionable spray fabric adhesive is a quick method as there are no pins or stitches to remove after quilting. Make sure your spray has been specifically designed to be used with fabric, as these won't damage your sewing machine and can be washed out after the quilt is finished.

Choose a space that is well ventilated. Spray your wadding/batting lightly on one side then lay your backing fabric on top, smoothing out any wrinkles as you go. Spray the wrong side of your quilt top and lay it centrally over the wadding/batting again, smoothing out any wrinkles or puckers. With larger quilts it may be easier to spray half or a quarter of the fabric at a time.

Try to avoid spraying the surrounding area. If you're concerned, lay down a few paper sheets around your quilt.

⊕ **Thread tacking/basting.** Many quilters prefer this method as you're automatically smoothing the fabrics as you sew. Cotton thread is most commonly used, although polyester thread is easy to pull through when removing the stitches. Water-soluble thread can also be used.

Use a long needle and a long piece of thread – that way, there is no need to knot. Start in the centre of your quilt and make large stitches to the outer edge of the quilt. Go back to the centre and sew to the opposite edge, then at 90 degrees. Continue across the quilt in this way to form a grid.

Some sewing machines have an extra long tacking/basting stitch, which you may find useful.

Curved safety pins are perfect for pinning together the layers of your quilt sandwich – the round shape can 'scoop' all the fabrics in one swoop.

⊕ Also available are **quilting tack guns.** These shoot a plastic tack through the layers of your sandwich which you then snip away with small scissors after quilting. Be careful not to sew through the tacks as this will damage your needle. The gun's nose may leave holes in fine fabrics.

⊕ **Fusible wadding/batting** is coated on each side with heat-sensitive glue that is activated by the steam from your iron, fusing all three layers together at once. **Fusible webbing or adhesive sheets** are a quick alternative if you have used a sew-in wadding/batting. Lay a piece of webbing or an adhesive sheet either side of the wadding/batting before pressing all three layers together.

STRAIGHT LINE QUILTING

Just as the name suggests, straight line quilting is sewing straight lines across your quilt. After creating your quilt sandwich, the time-consuming part is the marking of your quilt top (see also pages 22 and 23) to create guide lines you can follow when you begin to sew. For straight lines, you can use either a ruler and fabric marker pen or chalk; a seam guide on your machine (this slots into the back of your walking foot – see also page 15); or lay strips of masking or painter's tape across your quilt top and sew alongside them. (This is a quick way to quilt lines, but try not to catch the tape with your stitches – it can be difficult to remove from under the stitch! Guess how I found out…)

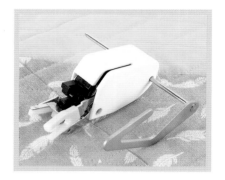

As alternatives to marking the fabric with a pen and ruler, use a seam guide (top) or lay strips of masking or painter's tape across your fabric and sew adjacent to them.

STRAIGHT LINE QUILTING IDEAS

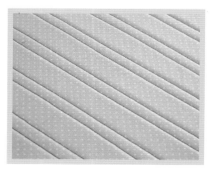

1 **Parallel straight lines**. Effective when quilted diagonally across the fabric.

2 **Cross-hatching**. Sew parallel straight lines in the opposite direction to the straight lines, seen left, to create a grid. Choose either 90- or 60-degree angles, depending on what suits your quilt design.

3 **Abstract**. If you're not too confident in sewing parallel straight lines, try drawing lines at angles to each other, creating an abstract effect.

QUILT-AS-YOU-GO

This is the perfect method for a beginner quilter or if you're short on space, as the blocks are made up into quilt sandwiches and quilted individually. You can create a large quilt without a bulk of fabric in your machine. If you're adding appliqué to your blocks, you'll find having a smaller area of fabric easier to pivot and turn.

Your blocks can be any size you like, be square or rectangular in shape, and can be made up into anything from coasters to bed quilts. The blocks can be simple patchworked panels; patchworked panels filled with embroidered designs – you could even quilt each block using different quilting techniques, treating them like samplers; panels with appliqué added to some or all of the blocks; or blocks using a mixture of all the above!

There are a couple of methods of joining your fabric pieces together. One is used for the Mini Chicken Quilt (see page 48); the other is to use pre-printed wadding/batting, seen below. To show you this process, I'm using a London Labyrinth block design with 12in (30.5cm) square blocks. Use a ¼in (5mm) seam allowance.

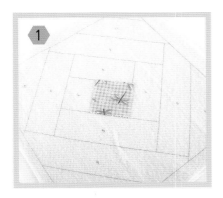
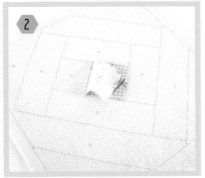
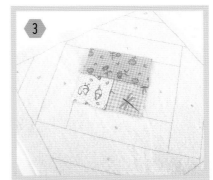

1 Following the manufacturer's instructions, cut out the required number of strips of fabric. This design happens to use a fabric roll. You may find it useful to number the strips with a fabric marker pen, to ensure they are placed correctly on the pre-printed wadding/batting. My first piece goes right in the centre and is secured with spray adhesive.

2 The second strip is sewn right sides together along one side.

3 Flip the fabric over and finger crease, then add the third piece in the same way, following the numbers on the wadding/batting or working around the central square clockwise.

4 Continue in this way until the whole area is covered. Repeat for all the blocks necessary to make your quilt, then trim the blocks to make them square.

To see how to sash your quilt-as-you-go block, turn to page 67.

FREE-MOTION EMBROIDERY

I really enjoy this embroidery technique – to add texture to my quilting projects, to attach appliqué shapes, to get creative with stitching artwork, but most of all, to have fun! Here's how it works.

44

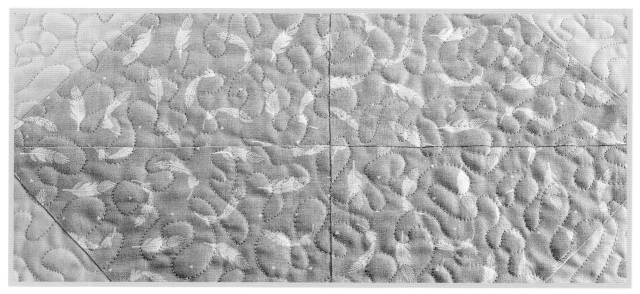

⊕ Think of your needle and thread as a pen and ink, but instead of moving the pen over the paper, you move the fabric under the needle to create your own unique designs. You will need a drop feed dog facility for your sewing machine (the feed dogs are the teeth that carry the fabric through the machine; by dropping these out of the way, you have control over moving the fabric in any direction you like) or a darning plate to cover the feed dogs, making them inactive. You'll also need a free-motion or darning foot. This foot 'hops' across the fabric, and allows you to see where you're stitching.

⊕ Have your machine set on a straight stitch with your needle in the centre position. The length of the stitch depends on how quickly you move your fabric – the quicker you move it, the longer the stitch you will sew. Place your hands either side of the needle, foot on the pedal and then off you go!

⊕ Try to keep the stitches as even as you can across the fabric. It's always helpful to practise first on scrap fabric.

⊕ Try to start sewing at the edge of your quilt to keep the ends of the thread out of the way.

⊕ On a large project, a full bobbin will mean less stopping!

⊕ If you do break a thread or need to refill the bobbin, take a needle and pull the bottom thread to the top (you may need to unpick a few stitches if the thread is too short). Loop the top and bottom threads together in a loose knot, place the needle through the loop and push the knot until it sits on the top of the fabric. Thread the ends through the needle, take the needle into the fabric just under the knot, and feed it in between the layers by about an inch (2.5cm), then bring it back to the top. Gently pull the thread until the knot pops inside the quilt and is hidden from view. Trim the thread.

Start sewing again one stitch back, taking your needle down and back up through the fabric. Then, with the presser foot raised, move your sewing away from the foot, pull on the thread tail and bring the bottom thread through to the top. Reposition your work to the first stitch and you're ready to go again. Avoid catching those loose threads – when you've finished sewing, you'll need to hide the starting threads again in the same way.

➕ Your quilting design can be anything you like – circles, swirls, geometric patterns or loose straight lines, there are no rules! But remember the point of quilting is primarily to hold the quilt sandwich together, so an even pattern with no large, unsewn areas works best. As a beginner you're probably not going to exhibit your work or put it into competitions, so please don't worry about perfection! You're meant to enjoy the sewing process, and nobody is going to notice the odd uneven or wobbly stitch!

➕ I like to use quilters' gloves. These are light-weight gloves with rubbery finger pads that help to grip the fabric. The gloves themselves also help to keep your quilt fabric clean!

➕ Slider mats are quite expensive but will make free-motion stippling a breeze! The mat is placed over the table of your sewing machine (see pages 12 and 13) and helps the fabric to glide easily under the needle, allowing you to move the fabric freely without friction!

➕ Posture is important, particularly when you're sewing for a while. Sit with your shoulders back and your elbows ideally at the same level as your machine. It's tempting to hunch your shoulders over your work, but you could suffer later! So, relax and enjoy the free-motion experience!

Top right: quilters' gloves.
Bottom right: slider mat.

FREE-MOTION QUILTING IDEAS

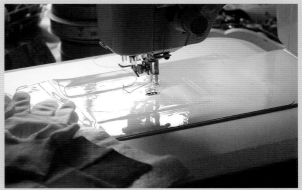

Stippling (sometimes called 'Vermicelli' quilting) is a free-motion, meandering design of wavy lines that traditionally don't overlap. If you're not too confident free-hand sewing a design like this, you can either draw it first or use a template. Use self-coloured thread to just add texture, or a contrast thread to really bring out the design. A variegated thread can really make a feature of the stitches.

If you have an all-over print on your fabric, try simply sewing around the outline of the print to quilt your project.

SELF-BOUND STRAIGHT BINDING

Self binding uses the backing fabric to create an effective bias binding-like border around the edge of the quilt. To achieve this, the backing fabric is cut larger than the quilt top and then folded over the edges. For example, to make a ½in (1.25cm) border, cut your backing fabric 1in (2.5cm) larger than your quilt top. Note that you'll need to move the backing fabric out of the way to trim the top fabric and wadding/batting when making them square (see page 40). There are a few ways to mitre the corners, so here are a couple.

46

Mitring self-bound corners — option 1

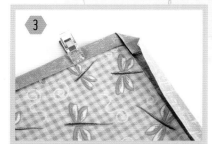

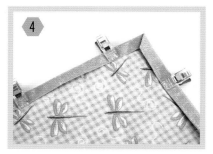

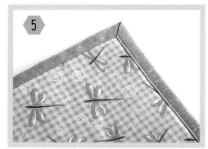

1 Fold one edge of backing fabric to meet the edge of the quilt top, then fold over again.

2 Take the folded edge at the point of the corner and fold at a right angle. Press.

3 Fold the next backing edge over to meet the edge of the quilt top.

4 Fold over again and you'll see a neat mitre in the corner.

5 Top-stitch close to the edge of the binding.

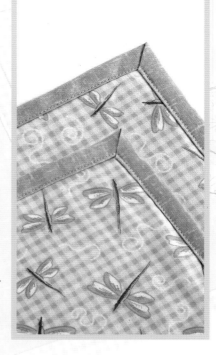

From top to bottom: larger backing piece behind the quilt top, ready for binding; the bound quilt from the front; and the bound quilt from the back.

Top: mitring option 1.
Bottom: mitring option 2.

Mitring self-bound corners – option 2

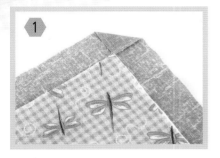

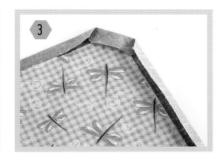

1 Fold over the corner of the backing fabric at a right angle, to meet the corner of the top. Crease.

2 Cut across the crease line. Fold the backing fabric over the corner of the fabric top and crease.

3 Fold the edges of the backing fabric over to meet the edge of the quilt top. Press.

4 Follow the same process in steps 4 and 5 on page 46 to form and secure the mitred corner. If you wish, you could sew the mitred corner by hand with ladder stitch. Here is the self-bound quilt from the back.

Project
MINI CHICKEN QUILT

Techniques

- Quilt-as-you-go
- Free-motion embroidery
- Appliqué
- Self-bound straight binding

Finished size

21 x 21in (53.5 x 53.5cm)

You will need

- 24in (61cm) square piece of top fabric, cut into nine 8in (20.5cm) squares
- 30in (76.25cm) backing fabric, cut into nine 10in (25.5cm) squares
- Nine 6 x 3in (15.25 x 7.75cm) pieces of appliqué fabric
- 30in (76.25cm) wadding/batting
- Fusible adhesive sheet
- Erasable marker pen
- Repositionable spray fabric adhesive
- Semi-circle template, for the chicken body (see page 93)

Notes

Use a ¼in (5mm) seam allowance.

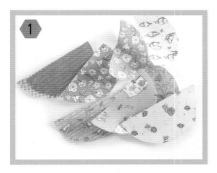

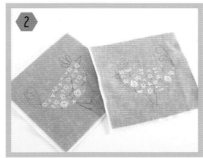

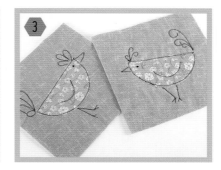

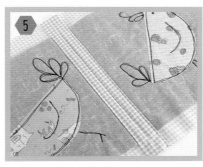

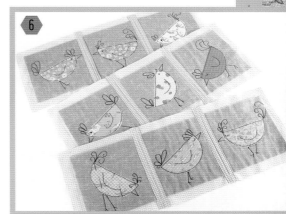

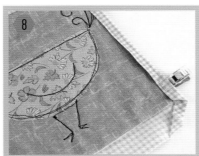

1 Fuse the adhesive sheet to the wrong sides of the appliqué fabric. Use your template to draw nine semi-circles onto the paper side of the sheets. Cut out the shapes.

2 Peel away the paper backings and iron the semi-circles to the centre of each top fabric square, at slightly different angles. With your erasable pen draw two stick legs, a curved line for a wing and a curly comb and tail onto and around each appliqué semi-circle – try to make each chick slightly different. Spray the wrong sides of the top fabric squares with respositionable spray fabric adhesive and place each square over the wadding/batting. Trim the wadding/batting around each individual square to approximately ½in (1.25cm) larger than the square.

3 Pop the free-motion/darning foot into your sewing machine and drop the feed dogs, then embroider over the markings drawn earlier, on all nine pieces. Try to avoid embroidering right up to the edge. These are your 'blocks'.

4 Take two of the backing squares and sew them right sides together, using a 1in (2.5cm) seam allowance. Press the seam open. Repeat to add a third block.

5 Spray the wrong sides of three of the chick blocks with spray adhesive then place each one onto the joined backing squares, lining up the edges to the stitch line of the seam. Fold the raw edges of the seams over to the right side of the blocks by ½in (1.25cm) then fold them over again by ½in (1.25cm). Top-stitch close to the folds.

6 Sew the remaining chick blocks and backing squares together in this way to make three rows of three.

7 Sew the three rows right sides together, using a 1in (2.5cm) seam allowance. As before, fold the backing fabric edges over the blocks twice and top-stitch close to the folds.

8 Mitre the outer corners: fold the backing fabric over the edge of the blocks and crease. Cut across the triangle to make the fold 1in (2.5cm) high. Fold the corners and side edges of the backing fabric over twice. You'll see mitres forming in the corner. Hand-sew the mitred corners in place with ladder stitch. Top-stitch all around the double-folded backing fabric edge to finish.

BIAS BINDING

Binding a project, whether it be a bed quilt or a tea cosy doesn't just finish the raw edge, it creates a neat frame to your work and adds another element of design. For a quilt, binding is often the final stage, after the sandwich has been quilted and trimmed. Fabric cut on the bias is slightly stronger than fabric cut on the grain and has a little 'give' too, so the fabric can stretch around curves or corners without puckering – this is especially helpful when mitring corners.

There are many ways of binding a quilt to give a professional finish, so firstly decide on the technique you'd like to use, the width of the binding and the colour of the fabric. If you decide not to make your own (see opposite), bias binding is available to buy in many colours, widths and prints. Single-fold bias tape will have the long edges pressed to the centre. Quilt binding is folded and pressed in half, with the raw edges together.

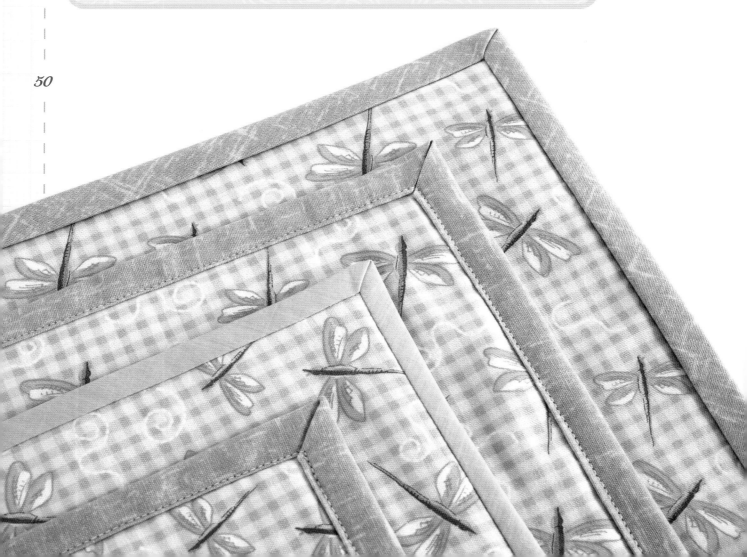

HAND-MADE BIAS BINDING

It's simple to make your own bias binding and this is often preferable when making a quilt; it means you can pick out specific prints and colours to either match or contrast with the colour palette you've chosen. If you're not sure which colours work best with your quilt, hang the quilt on a wall and offer up different colours – there are no rules, just choose whichever you think works best!

There is one clever little tool that is available to buy in many sizes, and is well worth the investment: a bias binding maker. You thread your bias-cut fabric strips into the gadget and it folds them ready for pressing, creating perfectly folded binding!

Bias binding maker.

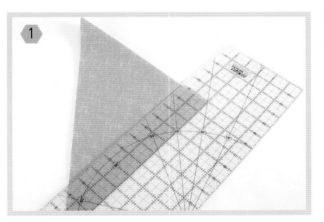

1 Decide on the width of binding you need, and if you want quilt or single-fold binding. Cut your fabric to twice the width you need, at a 45-degree angle to the selvedge/selvage.

2 To join lengths of binding, place two strips right sides together at right angles and overlapping slightly. Sew diagonally from the top left corner to the bottom right.

3 Trim the seam to ¼in (5mm) and press open.

4 If you are making quilt binding, simply press your bias-cut tape in half lengthways, raw edges together, using an iron. If you are making single-fold bias binding and you have a bias binding maker, thread your tape right side down through the bias binding maker, then pull the maker along the fabric as you press the folds with an iron.

ADDING SINGLE-FOLD BIAS TAPE

1 Trim your quilt to size, cutting through all three layers. Open out the bias tape and line up one long edge along the edge of the quilt top, right sides together. Sew along the crease, then stop at the corner of the quilt. The distance you stop from the edge should be the same as your seam allowance – for instance, if the crease line is ½in (1.25cm) from the edge, stop sewing ½in (1.25cm) from the edge of the quilt. Stop with the needle down, lift the presser foot and pivot the fabric. Continue to sew towards the corner and off the fabric.

2 Fold the bias tape around the corner, matching the edges – this should form a 'triangle' of binding at the corner.

3 Sew along the crease line of the next side, then repeat steps 1 and 2 to sew the other two corners and remaining sides. To join the ends of the binding, see opposite.

4 Fold the binding around the edge of the quilt, towards the backing fabric. Push out the corner – this will automatically form a mitre.

5 Arrange the mitre into the corner on the back of the quilt.

6 Sew the binding in place by hand with slip stitches, using the same colour thread as the binding to keep the stitches hidden and conceal the previous stitch line just under the binding.

Single-fold bias tape.

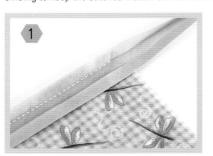

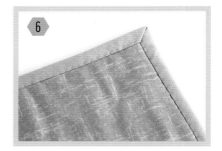

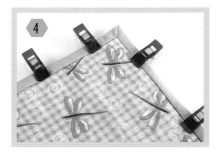

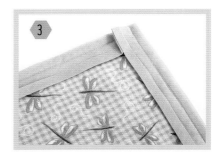

Tip
You could machine sew the binding in place, if you like, but the stitching will be more visible. I prefer to hand-sew as I like the stitches to be hidden, and I actually find hand-sewing really relaxing! If you're binding a large quilt, make sure you use a thimble!

Finished quilt from the front.

ADDING QUILT BINDING

1 My binding is a 3in (7.75cm) wide bias-cut strip of fabric folded in half – this will give me a ½in (1.25cm) border when finished. Trim your quilt. Sew the raw edges of the folded binding to the edge of the quilt with a ½in (1.25cm) seam allowance, right sides together. Stop sewing ½in (1.25cm) from the edge of the quilt, sew off the edge at an angle.

2 Take the binding around the corner, matching raw edges and forming a triangle in the corner. Sew along the edge, still using a ½in (1.25cm) seam allowance.

3 Fold the binding over to the back of the quilt and push out the mitred corner. Hand-sew as before.

Quilt binding.

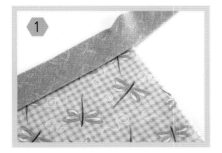

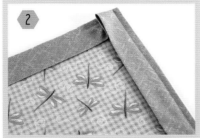

TO JOIN THE ENDS OF BIAS BINDING

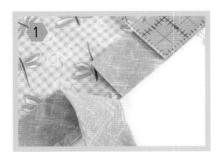

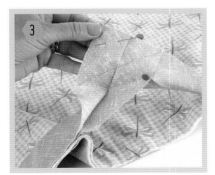

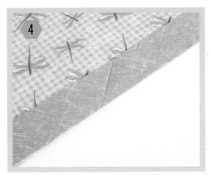

1 Pin the point where the seam will be. You'll find the seam less noticeable on the left-hand side of a quilt as the eye is automatically drawn to the centre and right of a project. Make sure your binding overlaps by about 5in (13cm) at each end. Sew around your quilt, leaving a generous opening. Overlap the pin with one end of the binding. Measure the width of the binding from the pin: my binding when folded is 1½in (4cm) wide, so I marked a line 1½in (4cm) from the pin.

2 Repeat with the second end, then trim the binding to the lines.

3 Open up the binding and pin right sides together at a right angle. Sew diagonally from corner to corner.

4 Remove the pins, trim the seam allowance and press. Sew the binding to the quilt.

Project
BEACH HUT HANGER

Techniques

- Patchwork
- Straight line quilting
- Free-motion embroidery
- Bias binding

Finished size

14 x 15in (35.5 x 38cm)

Note

Use a ¼in (5mm) seam allowance.

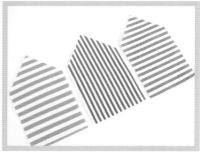

1 Fuse adhesive to the wrong sides of all of the appliqué fabrics (huts, roofs, doors, bunting, heart, yacht, clouds and sun). Take one hut piece, measure 2in (5cm) down from the top short edge and top sides, then cut at an angle to make a point at the top. Repeat with the other huts.

You will need

- ⊕ Beach –
  - Two 14 x 8in (35.5 x 20.5cm) pieces of yellow fabric
  - 14 x 8in (35.5 x 20.5cm) piece of foam stabilizer
  - 15in (38cm) length of 1in (2.5cm) wide yellow spotted bias binding, for the shoreline
  - Three 3½ x 6in (9 x 15.25cm) pieces of stripy fabric in different colours, for the huts
  - Six ½ x 3½in (1.25 x 9cm) strips of fabric in three different colours, for the roofs
  - Three 2 x 2½in (5 x 6.5cm) pieces of plain fabric in different colours, for the doors
  - Three small buttons
  - Scraps of coloured fabric, for the bunting and heart
- ⊕ Sea –
  - Two 14 x 11in (35.5 x 28cm) pieces of plain blue fabric
  - Three 1½in (4cm) square pieces of fabric in three colours, for the yacht
  - 15in (38cm) length of 1in (2.5cm) wide dark blue bias binding
  - 14 x 11in (35.5 x 28cm) piece of foam stabilizer

- ⊕ Sky –
  - 14 x 15in (35.5 x 38cm) piece of blue check fabric
  - 6 x 4in (15.25 x 10cm) piece of white fabric, for the clouds
  - 2in (5cm) square of yellow fabric, for the sun
  - 14 x 15in (35.5 x 38cm) piece of foam stabilizer
- ⊕ To hang –
  - 12 x 4in (30.5 x 10cm) piece of blue check fabric
  - 13in (33cm) length of ½in (1.25cm) wide wooden dowelling
  - 18in (45.75cm) length of cord
- ⊕ Also –
  - 14 x 15in (35.5 x 38cm) piece of backing fabric: I have used blue check fabric
  - 33in (84cm) length of 1in (2.5cm) wide yellow bias binding
  - 33in (84cm) length of 1in (2.5cm) wide pale blue bias binding
  - Fusible adhesive sheet
  - Erasable marking pen
  - Templates for the boat, sun, clouds, pennant triangles and door heart (see page 95)

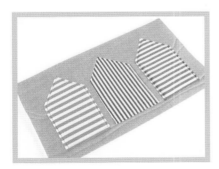

2 Fuse foam stabilizer to the wrong side of one yellow beach fabric piece. Arrange the huts over the right side of the stabilized fabric – make sure the appliqué pieces are not too close to the edges to allow for the bias binding. Peel away the paper backing and iron to adhere. Sew around the edges of the appliqué with straight quilting, with a ¼in (5mm) seam allowance, then free-motion embroider a few wavy lines in between the huts to create sand dunes. Stop sewing when you reach the appliqué, then take the thread through to the back and knot.

3 Peel and fuse the doors and roofs onto the huts, then straight line quilt around the edges with a ¼in (5mm) seam allowance. Draw a wavy line across the two end huts with your erasable marker pen. Cut the bunting scraps into small 1in (2.5cm) triangles, then adhere these along the line before sewing with a triple stitch on your machine. Sew a small heart above the door of the middle hut. Hand-sew a button 'handle' to each door.

4 Fuse foam stabilizer to the wrong side of one blue sea fabric piece. Place the sand section over the top of the sea, matching the bottom edges, and mark the position of the yacht, which should sit just on top of the sand piece. Remove the sand section then fuse the yacht in place. Sew around the edge of each yacht piece, then free-motion embroider wavy lines across the blue fabric to form waves.

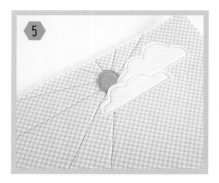

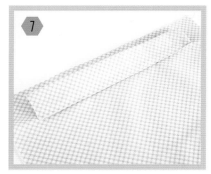

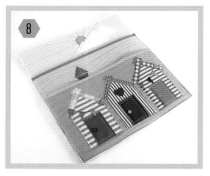

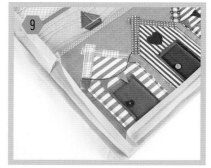

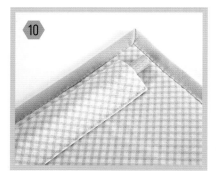

5 Cut out the sun and clouds from the yellow and white fabrics. Fuse foam stabilizer to the wrong side of one of the blue checked fabric pieces. Place the 'sea' over the 'sky' in the same way as you did the sand in step 4, and then mark the position of the sun and clouds. Remove the sea, adhere the sun and clouds then sew them in place. Draw 'rays' in straight lines from the sun, then sew to quilt.

6 Adhere the remaining yellow fabric to the back of the 'sand' piece, wrong sides together. Apply the yellow spotted bias binding across the top. Bind the 'sea' section in the same way, using the remaining blue fabric and dark blue bias binding.

7 Fold each short end of the 12 x 4in (30.5 x 10cm) strip of fabric to the wrong side by ½in (1.25cm) and press. Sew the two long edges right sides together to make a tube, then turn right side out and press. Sew the long bottom edge of this tube to the remaining blue checked fabric, 1in (2.5cm) down from the top with a ¼in (5mm) seam allowance.

8 Place the 'beach' on top of the 'sea', then place both over the 'sky'. Adhere the blue checked fabric to the back of the quilted front panel, wrong sides together, then sew all the way around through all the layers with a ¼in (5mm) seam allowance.

9 Apply the two different coloured bias bindings around the outer edge of the hanger: lay the plain yellow bias binding around the side and bottom edges of the 'sand' pocket first, right sides together, folding the short ends under by ¼in (5mm) to hide the raw edges. Sew along the crease to secure. Lay the pale blue bias binding along the edges of the sky and sea, the ends overlapping those of the yellow binding, then sew along the crease. Fold the joined binding over and sew in place as per steps 4 and 5 on page 52.

10 Thread the dowelling through the tube on the back, then tie the cord to either end of the dowelling to hang. What will you keep in yours?

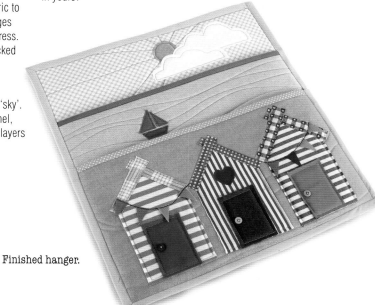

Finished hanger.

TRAPUNTO

Coming from the Italian 'to quilt', trapunto is a form of quilting that has extra wadding/batting under certain areas of the design to give it a 'stuffed' look. It has a luxurious, complicated appearance but is relatively simple to achieve.

Your design can be classic feathers or florals, through to words, birds or even cartoon characters – there are no rules!

1 The modern method for trapunto is to transfer your design first onto the right side of your project.

2 Place a couple of layers of wadding/batting behind the design. A high-loft type, such as polyester or polyester mix, makes the perfect padding material. Sew around the edge of the design with either a wash-away thread, or a contrast or co-ordinating thread. No backing fabric is needed at the moment.

3 Here's the design from the back.

4 Take a small pair of scissors – duck-billed scissors are useful as there's little chance of mistakenly cutting through the stitches – then trim the wadding/batting close to the stitched outline. Be careful not to snip through the fabric!

5 Place the fabric over a layer of wadding/batting, then place these in turn over a piece of tear-away stabilizer – this prevents too much lint from the wadding/batting going into your machine. Quilt the un-stuffed areas – I've used a small stippling stitch here. You will find closely spaced quilting lines help the design to stand out more. Either continue to stipple all over your work, or create an effective 'shadow' by just outlining the design.

6 Tear away the stabilizer. If you have used wash-away thread to outline your design, wash your work when it is finished to remove it.

Project
TRAPUNTO STOCKING

Techniques

- Trapunto
- Free-motion embroidery 'stippling' technique

Finished size

9 x 14in (23 x 35.75cm)

You will need

- 22 x 17in (56 x 43.25cm) piece of outer fabric
- 22 x 29in (56 x 73.75cm) piece of lining fabric
- 22 x 17in (56 x 43.25cm) piece of medium-loft wadding/batting
- 6 x 12in (15.25 x 30.5cm) piece of high-loft polyester wadding/batting
- 11 x 17in (28 x 43.25cm) piece of light-weight stabilizer
- 10in (25.5cm) length of ribbon or lace
- Pen and A3 (11¾ x 16½in) paper to make the pattern templates
- Adult sock, for the stocking template
- Erasable marker pen
- Repositionable spray fabric adhesive
- Stag template (see page 94)

Notes

Use a ¼in (5mm) seam allowance.

1 Make the stocking template by drawing around the sock with a 2in (5cm) border, as shown. Add an extra 2in (5cm) to the top edge. Cut out. Transfer the stag template onto paper and cut this out too.

2 Use the stocking template to cut out two outer and two lining fabric pieces. On the right side of one outer fabric piece place your stag template in the centre and then draw around it with an erasable marker pen – the top of the stag's head should be at least 4in (10cm) away from the top of the stocking.

3 Cut the 6 x 12in (15.25 x 30.5cm) piece of high-loft wadding/batting in half, then use a little spray adhesive to hold the two pieces together. Place your stag fabric over the top, so that the wadding/batting sits behind the marked area. Free-motion embroider around the outline of the stag.

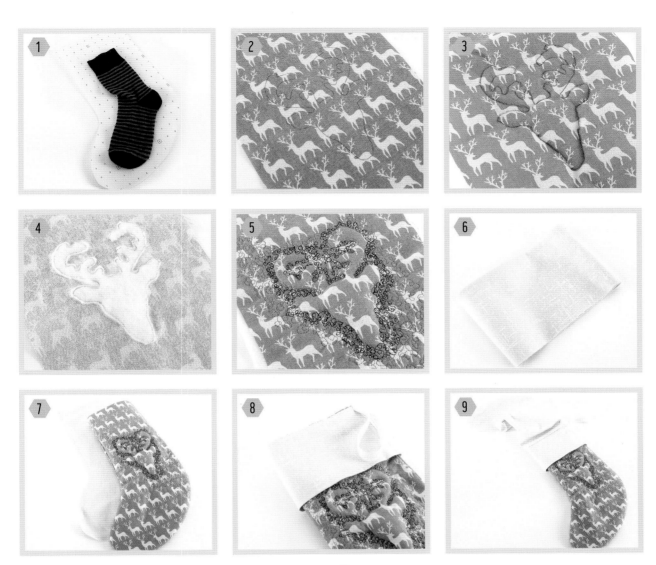

4 With a pair of duck-billed or small sharp scissors, snip away the wadding/batting close to the stitches.

5 Place the trapunto stag fabric over the top of one half of the medium-loft wadding/batting, and use a little spray adhesive to hold the two together. Cut around the wadding/batting, leaving a border of about ½in (1.25cm). Place this over the stabilizer, to prevent lint entering your machine when sewing. Free-motion embroider around the padded outline of the stag. I chose to sew in a diagonal line across my stocking, with small squiggly stitches that looped around the stag's head, then I went over the stitches with a darker colour, just around the head, to really make it stand out.

6 Measure the width of the top of your stocking – mine is 7in (17.75cm). Double the measurement then take away ½in (1.25cm) – that makes mine approximately 13½in (34.25cm). Cut a rectangle of lining fabric to this width, 7in (17.75cm) in height. Sew the short ends right sides together to make a 'tube'. Fold the top, short edge of the tube over to create a cuff. Top-stitch along the fold.

7 Fuse the remaining wadding/batting to the wrong side of the remaining outer fabric with adhesive spray and trim to size. Sew the two outer pieces right sides together, leaving the top open. Snip into the curves and turn the right side out. Sew the lining pieces together in the same way, this time leaving a turning gap of about 4in (10cm) in one side.

8 Place the cuff around the top of the outer stocking, with raw edges matching at the top and the seams matching at the side, as shown. Make a loop with your ribbon/lace and pin to the top edge, over the side seam. Tack/baste around the top, then remove any pins.

9 Drop the outer stocking inside the lining so that the right sides are together, then sew around the top. Turn the right side out through the gap in the lining and then machine sew the opening closed. Push the lining inside the stocking, fold over the cuff and press.

STITCH IN THE DITCH

Stitch in the ditch quilting is a method of sewing over an existing seam (the 'ditch') to create a barely visible stitch line, allowing the fabric and piecing of your project to be the main focus of the quilt. As the stitches are not meant to be seen, many quilters choose an invisible, monofilament thread to thread through their machine, or a colour thread that matches the fabric.

You can use a regular sewing machine foot or walking foot to stitch in the ditch, or you could invest in a stitch in the ditch foot, which has a blade-like guide along the centre.

Use your fingers to feel which way the seams have been pressed – one side of the fabric will be slightly raised, which creates the 'ditch' for you to sew along. When sewing, place your hands either side of the seam and gently pull them apart to open out the seam to give you a better guide line. As the stitches aren't creating a seam, it may be preferable to increase your stitch length to 3.

Do check the manufacturer's instructions on the packaging of your wadding/batting for a guide on how far apart to sew your seams, to make sure your quilt sandwich will hold together. The quilting distance can vary from 3in (7.5cm) to 10in (25.5cm), depending on the fibre content and how you're going to use your quilt. This isn't so important on smaller quilted projects, such as tea cosies or bags, as your quilting lines will be naturally closer together because of the size. However, if you have larger patchworked pieces you may need to add a few extra rows of stitches over your work to keep the quilt layers together.

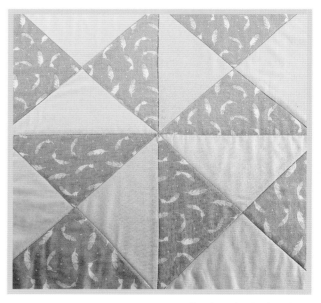

Stitch in the ditch quilting.

Stitch in the ditch foot – this has a blade-like guide at the centre of the foot, to guide your stitches along the ditch.

ADDING BORDERS

Some quilts won't need a border, but many quilt designs will benefit either from a plain or patterned border. Whichever style you choose, you will need to make joints at the corners. Here's a couple of the most popular ways.

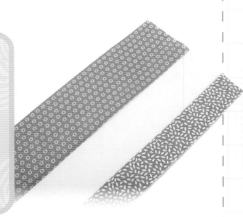

PIECED BORDERS

1 Decide on the width of your border strips – they can be as wide as you like! Measure the sides of your quilt then cut four strips, two to the exact length of the sides of the main quilt top, and the remaining top and bottom strips cut to the top and bottom lengths plus the strip width measurement at each end. This ensures the strips stagger along these sides.

2 Sew the two exact length border strips to their corresponding sides, right sides together and raw edges matching.

3 With the remaining longer strips, attach these to their corresponding sides in the same way as in step 2, this time centring them so that the longer ends overhang evenly at each end. They should butt against the shorter-length border strip, creating a neat 'pieced' edge. Press.

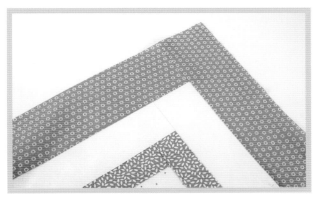

With the quilt above, I have added three borders around my central block design! For every set of borders, remember to remeasure your strips each time to ensure they overlap accurately at each end.

MITRED BORDERS

1 Sew as many strips as you need together for your border piece (I sewed three strips side by side for a tripled border) and press. The length of the border piece should be the length of the side of your main quilt design, plus enough for the border piece to overlap by its own width at either end, as in step 1 above. Sew the border strip centrally to the quilt top, right sides together, beginning and ending ¼in (5mm) from the corner. Repeat with the three remaining border pieces. Then, fold one corner of the quilt top at a 45-degree angle, so that the raw edges of the border match.

2 Draw a line across the border, extending from the fold of the quilt. If you have a few strips of fabric making up the border, as I have here, make sure to match the seams.

3 Sew along this drawn line then trim.

4 Remove any pins, open out and press. Repeat for the three remaining corners.

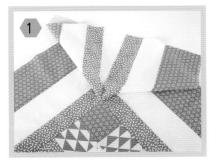

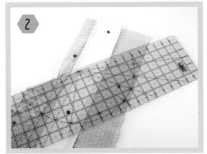

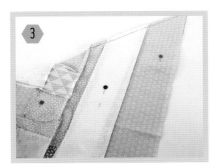

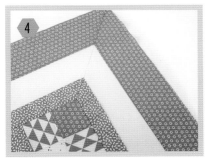

Project
TABLE RUNNER

Techniques

- Patchwork
- Free-motion embroidery
- Stitch in the ditch
- Adding borders
- Bias binding

Finished size

16 x 42in (40.75 x 106.75cm)

Notes

Use a ¼in (5mm) seam allowance.

You will need

- Six pieces of patterned fabric each measuring 22 x 10in (56 x 25.5cm): a fat quarter pack would be ideal, and you will have some scraps left over for other quilts!
- 20 x 46in (51 x 117cm) piece of backing fabric
- 46 x 15in (117 x 38.25cm) piece of plain fabric, for the border
- 20 x 46in (51 x 117cm) piece of wadding/batting
- 3⅜yd (3m) length of 1in (2.5cm) wide single-fold bias binding
- Repositionable spray fabric adhesive

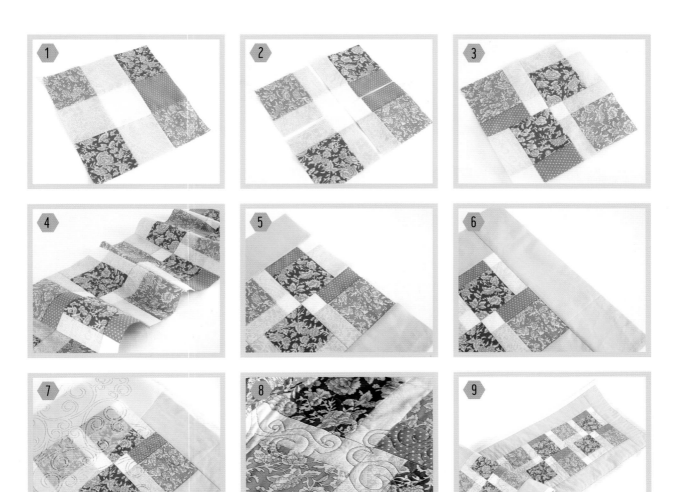

1 Cut your patterned fabric into 4in (10cm) squares. Arrange them into blocks of nine, each block in the same design, then sew together in rows, press, and then sew the rows together to make a block. Press again.

2 When you have four blocks, take each one and cut in half, then half again to quarter.

3 Now it's play time! Turn two opposite squares around, or try rotating all four pieces – you'll see different patterns developing. I turned the top right and bottom left squares by 90 degrees. When you're happy with the design, sew the four pieces right sides together, matching the points in the centre. Press.

4 Sew all four blocks together in a row, again making sure the points match. Trim the edges if necessary.

5 Cut the border fabric into 4in (10cm) wide strips. Sew two strips right sides together to the long sides of the runner. Press.

6 Sew two strips right sides together to the short sides. Press again.

7 Choose how you're going to quilt your runner – I've used a stencil (see also page 23), so have transferred the markings with an air-erasable pen. Place your quilt top over the wadding/batting, then place both these layers over the wrong side of the backing fabric. As this is quite a small project, I've used repositionable spray fabric adhesive to hold the layers together; however, you could pin or tack/ baste if you prefer.

8 Free-motion embroider over the markings, then stitch in the ditch around the border. Trim the outer edges of the whole panel to make a 3½in (9cm) wide border.

9 Apply bias binding all the way round (see pages 50–53).

Project
QUILTED TOTE

Techniques

- Straight line/cross-hatch quilting
- Free-motion embroidery

Finished size

11 x 15in (28 x 38cm)

You will need

- 12 x 20in (30.5 x 52cm) piece of plain fabric
- 30½ x 24in (77.5 x 61cm) piece of patterned fabric
- 24 x 17in (61 x 40.75cm) piece of fusible wadding/batting
- Erasable marker pen and ruler
- 6in (15.25cm) length of ribbon
- One button, to match the ribbon

Notes

Use a ¼in (5mm) seam allowance.

1 Cut the following from your fabrics: two plain pieces measuring 12 x 10in (30.5 x 25.5cm), two patterned pieces measuring 12 x 4in (30.5 x 10cm) and two patterned pieces measuring 12 x 3in (30.5 x 7.5cm). Place the longer patterned pieces to the bottoms of the plain panels and the shorter patterned pieces to the tops of the plain panels as shown. Sew them in place, right sides together, and press.

2 Top-stitch along each side of the seams. Then take your marker pen and ruler and draw a line straight down the centre of the plain section. From this central line draw parallel lines at 1½in (4cm) intervals across the fabric. Repeat the process crosswise across the plain fabric to create a grid.

3 Adhere your wadding/batting to the wrong sides of both outer pieces and trim. Sew along the grid lines – you may wish to increase the length of your stitch (I'm using a 3mm stitch length). Mark the boxes you're going to embroider: for my tote, I've chosen random boxes with no particular pattern in mind.

4 Pop your free-motion embroidery foot onto your machine, drop the feed dogs and sew over the marked boxes. I've sewn a diagonal, meandering line from one side of the box to the other. Alternatively, you could try a very small stippling stitch. These are the outer bag pieces.

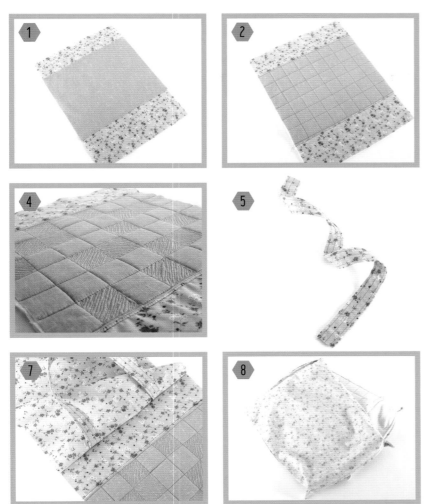

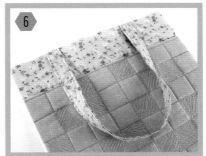

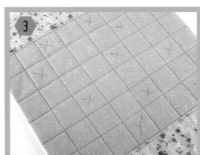

5 To make the handles, cut two strips of patterned fabric measuring 18 x 4in (45.75 x 10.25cm). Fold one handle in half lengthways, wrong sides together, and press. Open out the fabric, fold the two long sides to the centre and press again. Fold the whole handle in half again and press. Finish the handle by sewing along each long side then down the centre. Repeat with the remaining handle strip.

6 Pin then tack/baste the handles to the top of each side of the bag, raw edges matching and the loop of the handle facing downwards. Check they're not twisted! Remove the pins.

7 Cut two patterned pieces measuring 12 x 15½in (30.5 x 39.5cm) to make the lining panels. Sew a lining piece right sides together to the top of each outer bag piece, sandwiching the handles in between the two layers.

8 Pin outer to outer and lining piece to lining piece, right sides together and matching the seams. Sew along the bottom and sides of each bag section, leaving a turning gap in one side of the lining of about 4in (10cm). Pinch each bag corner in turn, so that the side seam sits over the base seam (you will be able to feel this with your fingers). Mark a line 1in (2.5cm) from each point and sew across. This will create a narrow boxed base for the outer and lining bags.

9 Turn right side out through the gap in the lining and machine sew the opening closed. Push the lining inside the bag, press then top-stitch around the top of your tote. Fold the ribbon in half and hand-sew to one side of the tote. Cover the fold and stitching with the matching button to finish.

SASHING

Sashing is technically a patchwork technique, and is a way of piecing strips of fabric to frame each block in your quilt.

Not all quilts need sashing, and it shouldn't outshine the blocks, but it is a useful addition to a quilt, especially one with patchwork. Busy-patterned blocks can be separated with sashing, to prevent the designs running into each other, and wide sashing can quickly make a small quilt much larger. If the same colour as the background of your blocks is used, it really makes your patchworked areas stand out.

Here are two methods of adding sashing.

REGULAR SASHING

The width of the sashing depends on the look you're creating and the size of your blocks. Try laying out the blocks first with different-sized spaces and decide which works best for your quilt. If you need to join the sashing pieces, do so with a diagonal seam (as with bias binding, see page 53) to make the join less visible.

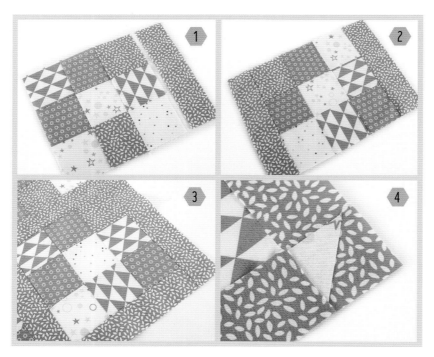

1 Measure the height of your blocks then cut as many strips of sashing to this length as you require.

2 Sew the strips either side of the first block, right sides together. Sew sashing strips to the right-hand side of each other block in the row in the same way. Join the blocks together then press towards the strips.

3 When your rows are completed, measure the length of the rows and cut strips to this length. These are sewn to the rows of blocks in the same way.

4 You could also create decorative sashing by adding squares (known as 'cornerstones') adjacent to the quilt blocks, which in turn can be made up of squares, half- or quarter-square triangles.

5 Create your quilt sandwich, as per page 40.

QUILT-AS-YOU-GO SASHING

Sashing for quilt-as-you-go projects is different to regular quilts, as the blocks are already quilted through all three layers.

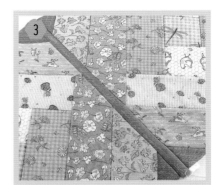

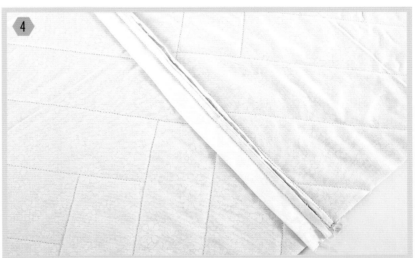

1 Begin by cutting a top sashing strip measuring 1in (2.5cm) wide. The length should be the size of your block, plus a little extra – for example, my blocks are 12in (30.5cm) square, so I cut my sashing 13in (33cm) long. For the strip of sashing on the back of the block, cut a strip to the same length but this time measuring 1¾in (4.5cm) wide. Fold this back sashing strip in half lengthways, wrong sides together, and press.

2 Place the top sashing strip to one side of the block, right sides together and avoiding any edges that will be around the outside edge of the quilt. The folded backing strip goes onto the underside of the block, right sides together and raw edges matching. The block should be sandwiched in-between the two sashing pieces.

3 Sew the remaining raw edge of the top sashing strip to the next block, right sides together. Take care you don't sew through to the back sashing strip.

4 You'll see on the back of the quilt that the edges of the two blocks meet...

5 ... Fold the backing strip over the seam and hand-sew with slip stitch. When your blocks are completed in horizontal strips, apply the sashing across the top and bottom in the same way again, avoiding the outer edges of the quilt.

6 Bind the quilt with bias binding (see page 52) – I have used single-fold bias tape.

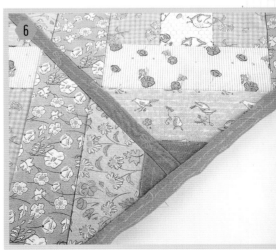

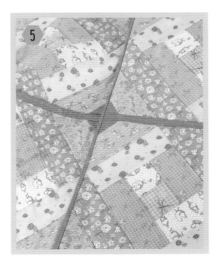

Project
BUNTING QUILT

Techniques

- Patchwork
- Free-motion embroidery 'stippling' technique
- Sashing
- Adding borders
- Bias binding

Finished size

35 x 53in (89 x 134.75cm)

You will need

- 45 x 38in (1.25 x 1m) piece of patterned fabric, for the pennants: you may need less if you have a non-directional print
- 45 x 12in (125 x 30.5cm) strip of plain fabric, for the strips: mine has a denim effect
- 45 x 60in (1.25 x 1.5m) piece of white fabric, for the quilt top
- 45 x 60in (1.25 x 1.5m) piece of white fabric, for the quilt back
- 45 x 60in (1.25 x 1.5m) piece of natural wadding/batting
- 5yd (4.5m) length of 1in (2.5cm) wide single-fold bias binding
- Triangle template (see page 92)

Notes

Use a ¼in (5mm) seam allowance.

1 Use the template to cut thirty-five triangles from patterned fabric and forty triangles from the white fabric. Cut five strips from the plain length of fabric measuring 2 x 44in (5 x 111.75cm), six white strips measuring 4 x 44in (10 x 111.75cm) and two white strips measuring 4 x 60in (10 x 152.5cm) – you will need to join the fabric.

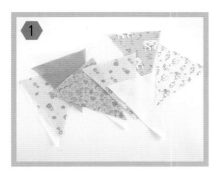
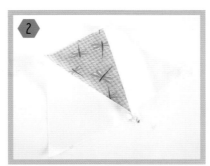

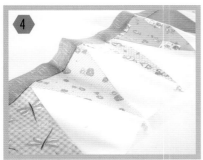
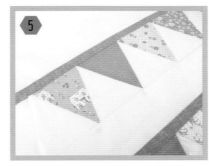
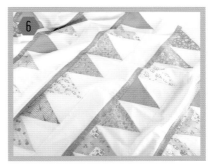

2 For each row, you'll need seven patterned alternating with eight white triangles, so that you will finish with a white triangle on each end. It may help to lay all the pieces out first before sewing. Sew the triangles right sides together – as you match the raw edges, slide the fabric to leave ¼in (5mm) of the triangle overhanging at each end. A quarter-inch presser foot will be handy here, if you have one.

3 When you have your five rows of alternating pennants with a white on each end, press the seams in the same direction. (If your coloured fabric shows through the white, press towards the darker seam.)

4 Sew a 2 x 44in (5 x 111.75cm) strip of plain coloured fabric to the top of each row of pennants, right sides together. Press as you go.

5 Sew a 4 x 44in (10 x 111.75cm) white strip to the top of each plain strip, right sides together. Press as you go. When all five rows of bunting are complete, join them together.

6 Sew the final white strip to the bottom, right sides together, then add the two long strips at each side in the same way to create a border.

7 Place the quilt top over the wadding/batting, then over the wrong side of the backing fabric. Pin or tack/baste together, as you prefer. If using pins, place them in the centre of the pennants as these areas aren't sewn. Sew a running stitch around each pennant in a contrasting thread, then put your free-motion foot on your sewing machine and stipple over the white fabric – I've used geometrical shapes as I thought it worked well with triangles!

8 Trim the edges then apply bias binding (see pages 50–53).

Tip
The easiest and quickest way to cut out your triangles is to cut out the triangle template from card (cereal box card will do!), then layer up the fabrics and use a rotary cutter, ruler and mat to cut out several triangles at a time.

Project
BARGELLO PILLOWCASE

Techniques

- Patchwork
- Straight line quilting OR stitch in the ditch

Finished size

25½ x 18½in (64.75 x 47cm)

Notes

Use a ¼in (5mm) seam allowance.

You will need

- Ten 2½ x 44in (6.5 x 111.75cm) strips of fabric – one very dark, one very light, then two of each of the two shades in between. Pre-cut strips are ideal, as the fabric colour will already work!
- Two 20 x 18in (51 x 45.75cm) pieces of fabric, for the backing: mine has a bird and twig pattern
- Two 10 x 18in (25.5 x 45.75cm) pieces of fabric, for the backing: mine is black abstract
- 26 x 20in (66 x 51cm) piece of wadding/batting
- 28 x 22in (71.25 x 56cm) piece of lining fabric: mine is cream cotton
- Three buttons
- 25 x 16in (63 x 40cm) pillow insert
- Ruler and erasable marker pen: I actually used chalk for my pillowcase, as it stood out on the colour of my fabric

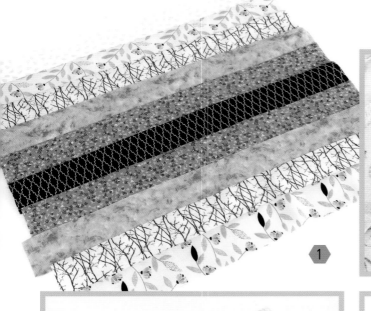

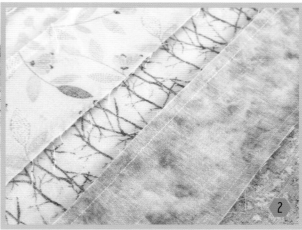

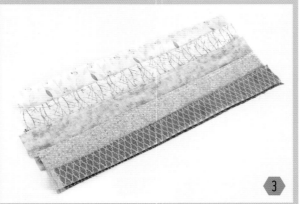

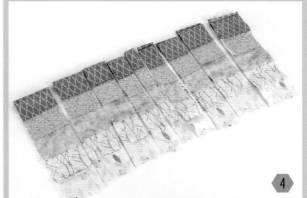

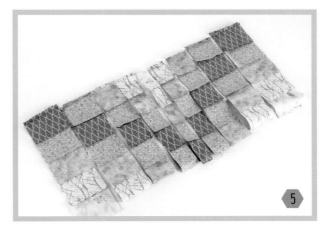

1 Cut your ten fabric strips in half widthways, so that the strips are still 2½in (6.5cm) wide. Place the darkest strip in the centre, then lay the next darkest strips either side. Continue working outwards, with the colour strips getting lighter and finishing with the lightest colours. The tenth and final lightest strip goes on one side only. The strips will be sewn together to make a tube, so take care that you don't have the same colours on each end to avoid having two blocks of the same colour next to each other. Sew the strips right sides together with a ¼in (5mm) seam allowance.

2 Press the seams to one side, each seam in the opposite direction to the previous one.

3 Sew the two long ends together to make a tube.

4 Trim one end of the tube to make a straight edge. From this edge, use your rotary cutter and ruler to cut your tube into 'rings'. They should measure: 3in (7.5cm), 2½in (6.5cm), 2in (5cm), 1½in (3.75cm), 1in (2.5cm), 1½in (3.75cm), 2in (5cm), 2½in (6.5cm) and 3in (7.5cm).

5 Use your quick unpick to undo the stitches at the top of the first ring. Roll the second ring so that the next colour comes to the top, undo the stitches again. Continue in this way until the colour you started with is at the bottom – this should be the narrowest strip. Now roll in the opposite direction, unpicking the stitches as you go, to graduate to the first colour back to the top.

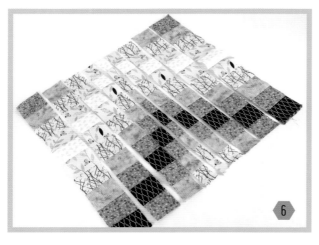

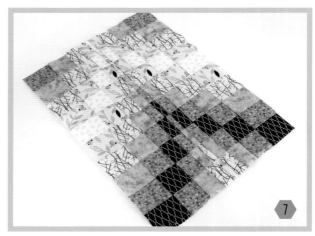

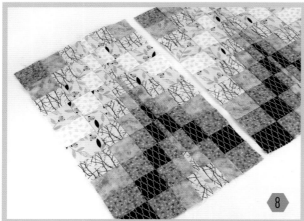

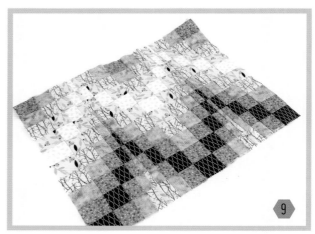

6 Open out the strips and you'll see the wave effect.

7 Sew these strips together with a ¼in (5mm) seam allowance, matching the seams. As you've pressed them in opposite directions, the seams should butt together easily. Press all the new seams to one side.

8 Repeat with the second set of fabric strips, leaving off one of the 3in (7.5cm) strips at one side. When you place the two sections together, there should be a single 3in (7.5cm) strip in the centre.

9 Sew the two sections right sides together. Press.

10 Mark your quilting lines over the top of the fabric. I've chosen simple curved lines that follow the lines of the blocks, but you could just stitch in the ditch if you prefer. Place the fabric panel over your wadding/batting, then turn over your lining fabric to form your 'quilt sandwich'. Sew along the lines. Once you have finished quilting, remove your marked lines, trim the wadding/batting and lining to the fabric then square off.

11 Sew your 20 x 18in (51 x 45.75cm) fabric pieces right sides together along one 18in (45.75cm) edge. Fold over and press, then top-stitch along the seam. Repeat with the remaining fabric pieces.

12 Place the larger fabric piece right sides together with the patchworked side, raw edges matching, then place the smaller piece over the opposite end so that they overlap. Sew all the way around. Finish the seams with an overedge or zigzag stitch. Turn right side out and hand-sew your decorative buttons in place to the top side of the envelope closure. Insert pillow pad to finish.

Finished pillow cover.

ECHO QUILTING

This is a simple technique of outlining or sewing inside blocks or appliqué shapes either by hand or machine. It gives a very modern look to your work and is a great way of filling empty spaces.

The outlines don't necessarily need to be marked out, making this a quick method of adding texture and interest to your quilt. If you're machine sewing this can be done using either your quarter-inch foot or the edge of your standard or walking foot. When pivoting around corners and curves, leave the needle in the 'down' position so that your stitch line is fluid. Many machines have a 'needle up/down' function, which is invaluable in this case. However, if you are sewing lots of curves and angles on your sewing machine, try free-motion embroidery with a free-motion foot.

Sew as many echoing lines as you like – you can fill in the whole space or simply create a couple of outlines.

74

A quarter-inch, standard or walking foot is perfect for angular outlines (below left), but more complex and unusual shapes (below right) or ones with curves are more easily sewn with a free-motion foot.

TYING A QUILTERS' KNOT

This is the easiest and quickest knot I've ever tied! This method makes a neat knot at the end of your thread, and I have used it for all the hand-sewn projects in this book.

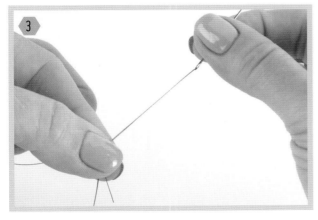

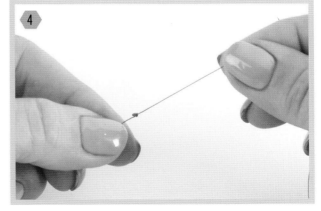

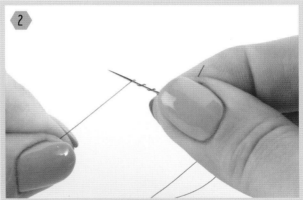

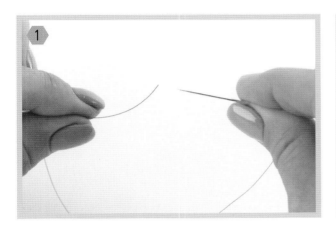

1 Thread your needle then take the end of the thread to the point of the needle.

2 Overlap the two, then wrap the thread around the needle three or four times – the more wraps, the larger the knot will be.

3 Hold on to the wrapped threads and pull the needle through. Take the wrapped threads to the end of the thread.

4 You'll have a neat little knot!

ENGLISH PAPER PIECING

Often known by quilters as EPP, this is a method of wrapping fabric around paper shapes and hand-sewing the edges of these shapes together to create accurate, regular seams and intricate designs.

This technique dates back to the early eighteenth century, and the oldest surviving example is found on a quilt in the United States dating from the late 1700s. As paper was hard to come by in those days, old letters or newspaper was used and re-used; nowadays, you can buy template shapes or make your own. If you're making your own templates, I'd suggest you use a paper with a minimum of 160gsm (110lb); this is thin enough to sew through yet firm enough to give structure and stability to the fabric that you'll wrap around it. The paper shapes are then removed after sewing and can be re-used.

Traditional shapes for EPP are the ever-popular hexagon, half hexagon (shown top right), triangles, diamonds and squares; more modern designs include tumblers (shown second from top), jewels, clam shells and apple cores (shown third from top) and houses (shown bottom). Different shapes can be used together to create hundreds of different patterns, and a clever use of colour can trick the eye into seeing three-dimensional designs.

Sewing fabric pieces together in this way may be time consuming, especially as almost all of your design will be hand-sewn, but this technique does have its benefits. Your 'Y' seams and points should be perfect, as I find hand-sewn pieces so much easier to make accurate than machine sewing. You also don't need to worry about seam allowances when joining the shapes. Lastly, this is repetitive, quiet stitching that doesn't take up much space, making it a perfect relaxing pastime for sewers on the go!

EPP templates.

76

Tip
Some fabrics will form little 'ears' when folded around the paper shapes, don't cut these off! They help the pieces to sit together.

THE BASIC TECHNIQUE

There are a few different techniques for sewing the pieces together, depending on the shape you're using, but essentially this is the way it works:

1 Cut your fabric ¼in (5mm) larger than your template – this measurement doesn't have to be exact.

2 Place the template in the centre of the wrong side of your fabric, then wrap the fabric around the template and secure. There are three ways to do this:

The first technique is to tack/baste by hand, sewing straight through the fabric and paper with large stitches (A). These stitches will be removed when the patchwork pieces have been sewn together.

The second option is to tack/baste by hand, just catching the corners of the fabric without taking the needle through the paper (B). Using this method means you won't need to remove the stitches when your work is complete.

The final method which I like is to use a fabric glue stick (C). When I took a quilting course many years ago, my tutor was quite shocked when I suggested using glue! Nowadays it's quite acceptable, and can save a lot of time, particularly with larger projects.

3 Take a length of thread around 12in (30.5cm) in length. Hold two fabric pieces right sides together, knot the end of your thread (see technique on page 75) and take the needle through the very edge of your fabric pieces, catching just a couple of threads (A). Try to skim the needle across the edge of the paper template, but don't worry if it touches the paper – you'll still be able to re-use it. Use an overedge stitch, which means taking the thread over the folded edges of the pieces, and keep the stitches close together. Aim for 12 stitches to an inch – the smaller the stitches the less visible they will be, and will create a stronger seam (B).

4 Although it's not necessary to cut your thread before moving onto the next fabric piece, I like to make a secure knot at the end of each piece, just to make sure it won't come undone! When you've sewn together a few pieces, press from the back with a dry iron, then carefully remove the papers, making sure the outer pieces remain in place until your EPP is complete.

⊕ A 12in (30.5cm) length of thread works best for EPP. If your thread is too long it may knot, or become weak as it is dragged across the edge of the paper.

⊕ Choose a thread that is slightly darker in colour than your fabric. If you have a patterned fabric, a grey or beige thread will blend well with all colours.

⊕ Don't be tempted to use poor quality thread – weak thread creates a weak seam and it would be a shame if your stitches were to break after all your hard work!

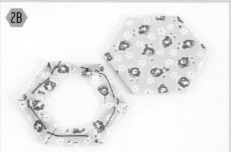

Project
SNOWFLAKE PLACEMAT

Techniques

- English paper piecing
- Echo quilting
- Bias binding

Finished size

13 x 13in (33 x 33cm)

You will need

- 14 x 28in (36 x 72cm) piece of white-on-white fabric
- 14in (36cm) square of wadding/batting
- 12 x 7in (31 x 18cm) piece of light grey fabric
- 10 x 6in (25.5 x 15.25cm) piece of dark grey fabric
- 20 x 5in (51 x 13cm) piece of light blue fabric
- 56in (1.4m) of ½in (1.25cm) wide single-fold bias tape
- Paper, to make the EPP templates
- Repositionable spray fabric adhesive
- EPP templates (see page 94)

Notes

Use a ¼in (5mm) seam allowance.

To help you echo quilt an accurate ¼in (5mm) outline around your motif, you could use a quarter-inch presser foot.

Tip
This would also create a very pretty quilt block!

1 Using the templates, transfer five large, ten medium and five small kite shapes and one circle template onto the paper. Use the templates to cut out your fabric, adding a ¼in (5mm) seam allowance on all sides. For the large kite shapes use the light grey fabric; use blue for the medium kites and dark grey for the small kites. Wrap the corresponding fabric around the paper pieces and either tack/baste or glue in place (see 'English Paper Piecing' on page 76).

2 Hand-sew the pieces right sides together using tiny overedge stitches – the order is large, medium, small, medium, large and so on.

3 Continue until you have completed a circle. Take a running stitch around the edge of the circle shape's fabric, place the paper in the centre and pull your thread to gather. Press.

4 Place the circle in the centre of the snowflake and sew in place with slip stitch. Press the whole snowflake, then carefully remove the papers. Cut your white-on-white fabric in half to make two squares. Spray the back of the snowflake with repositionable adhesive and place in the centre of one of the squares. Stitch around the edge of the snowflake to secure it in place with your sewing machine.

5 Place the two squares wrong sides together, sandwiching the wadding/batting between them. Sew around the circle then twice around the outside of the snowflake – the outlines are ¼in (5mm) apart, as shown. Trim to make square, then apply bias binding around the edge (see page 52), mitring the corners as you sew.

BAG MAKING

A bag or purse is a perfect quilting project for the beginner: you can use and practise your quilting skills, and it is relatively quicker to make a bag compared to making a bed quilt. I think handbags benefit from metal hardware to give them a shop-bought look, but many fastenings don't come with instructions. Here are a few pointers.

Example of a bag with quilted features. The bag's front pocket has quilted diamonds, with an appliqué detail finished off with satin stitch edging.

FITTING MAGNETIC SNAPS

I'd recommend placing a scrap of fabric behind the snap, on the wrong side of your fabric, to stabilize the fabric and help to stop the snaps pulling. If you're fitting to a bag with a flap, the narrower side of the snap will go onto the flap and the wider section onto the bag.

The snaps come in two halves with a disc-shaped back section for each side.

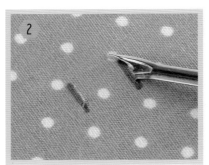

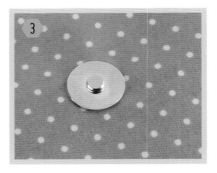

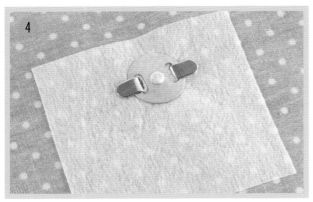

1 Mark the position of the snap with an erasable marker pen, placing the back of the snap on your fabric and drawing through the two long holes either side of the central hole.

2 Take your seam ripper or a small pair of sharp scissors and make a small incision over the long lines. It's better to make the cuts too small so they can be made bigger. If you cut them too big you may ruin your project.

3 Push the prongs of the snap through the holes.

4 Open out the prongs on the back of the fabric. It doesn't really matter whether you open them outwards or close them inwards. Personally I find them easier to open outwards. Repeat for other half of the snap.

FITTING SNAP FASTENERS

Always follow the manufacturer's instructions with the snap fastener kits that you buy, but if you're a little confused, this is how the basic kits work.

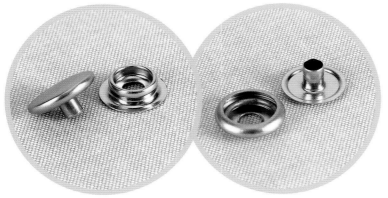

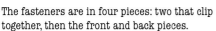

The fasteners are in four pieces: two that clip together, then the front and back pieces.

You'll have a tool with a hole in one end, to cut the hole in your fabric. You'll also have a tool with a pointed end which you'll use to fix two pieces together.

1 Make sure you're working on a solid base; most kits will provide a hard disc to hammer into. Make a mark on your fabric where you want the fastener to go. Place the hole end of the small tool over the mark, and tap with a small hammer until you go through the fabric.

2 Push the 'stalk' of the domed side of the fastener through the hole.

3 Turn over, and place the shallow side of the inside of the fastener over the 'stalk'. The pointed tool goes into this stalk, and again, tap with the hammer. The stalk will split, curling over the sides to attach both sides together. Hammer until the fastener feels secure.

4 Repeat with the opposite sides of your fastener.

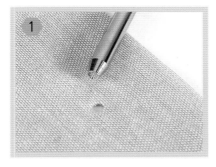

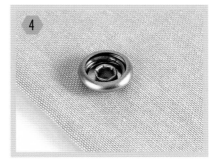

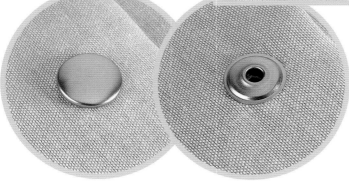

Far left: this is how the fastener should look from the front when closed.

Left: this is how the fastener should look from the back.

HAND QUILTING

Straight line, cross-hatch, echo quilting or using stencils – all of these quilting techniques can be hand-sewn. It takes longer than machine sewing, but it's a perfect way to relax without the noise of a sewing machine and the results are worth the time taken.

⊕ Ideally your stitches should be uniform, measuring ¼in (5mm) in length or smaller. If your work is being judged in a quilt show it's expected that your stitches are small and even on both sides of your work. However, for your own quilt, size and uniformity of the stitches is entirely up to you. Personally, I like to see a few uneven stitches as I think it adds personality to your quilt, and shows that it really has been hand-quilted! If it's important for you to achieve perfection then take your time and practise. If not, then just enjoy the process and be proud of your work no matter how uneven your stitches are!

⊕ A few things you'll need for the best results are **hand-quilting thread**, **betweens**, a **hoop or frame** and a **thimble**.

⊕ Hand-quilting thread is quite heavy and is coated to enable the thread to travel through your quilt sandwich easily. Alternatively, try waxing your thread using a beeswax block.

⊕ Betweens are the needles of choice for hand quilting. They are quite small in length and are narrow, but do come in different sizes. The larger the number of the needle, the smaller it is. To start with, try a size 10 or 12.

⊕ Use a large embroidery hoop for small projects. Quilting hoops are available for larger projects, which are deeper than embroidery hoops making them stronger and able to take the weight of fabric. Also available are lap and floor frames. Like the hoops, a lap frame is ideal for smaller, on-the-go designs; floor frames are perfect for larger quilts.

⊕ Of course, you will definitely need a thimble! I like to use a leather thimble for hand quilting, but you may find a metal or rubber one easier to use. It's your choice!

82

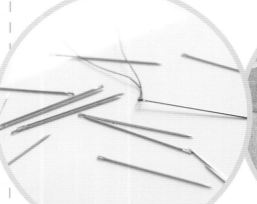

THE BASIC TECHNIQUE

1 After constructing your quilt sandwich, mark out your pattern. This could be using a stencil or a freehand design. Place your fabric into a frame or hoop but, unlike embroidery, don't have the fabric taut.

2 Tie a small quilters' knot at the end of the thread (see technique on page 75). Insert your needle into your work from the top, around ½in (1.25cm) from where you want to start quilting. Bring the needle up again at the point where you'll begin.

3 Tug the thread sharply to pull the knot inside the wadding/batting and hide it.

4 You can start by just sewing individual stitches. Pop on your thimble and take the needle through from the front to the back of the quilt sandwich to start making a running stitch.

5 When you gain a bit more confidence, you can take several stitches onto the needle by inserting the end into your work with one hand and feeling with your second hand, under the work, where the needle comes through by ¼in (5mm) – or the length of stitch you require. Rock the needle backwards and bring through to the top, then repeat until you have three or four stitches on your needle. At this point you can undo them if they don't look even enough. Pull the needle through and repeat!

6 When you come to your final stitch, with the needle and thread on top of your work, tie a small knot ½in (1.25cm) from the point where the thread comes through the fabric.

7 Take the needle through to the wrong side of the quilt to create the last stitch, and gently tug the knot into the wadding/batting to hide it, just as you did at the start.

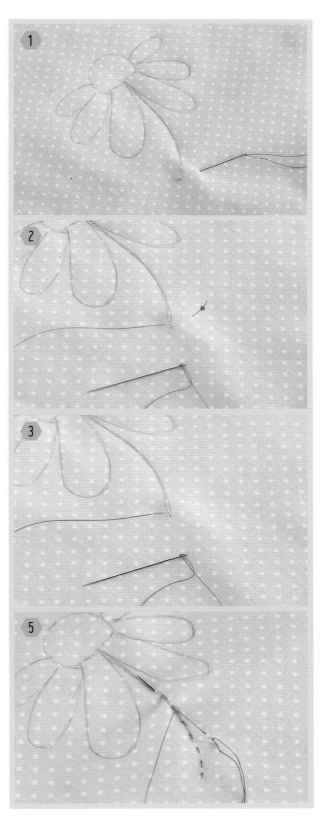

Finished hand-quilted design.

BIG STITCH QUILTING

Big stitch quilting is exactly that – quilting with big stitches! The difference isn't just in the size of the stitches, it's also the needle and thread used. To create these very noticeable stitches, use a thicker, decorative or embroidery thread/floss and a big stitch or embroidery needle.

Embroidery threads/floss.

1 Thread your needle and knot the end (see the technique on page 75). Take the needle into the quilt approximately ½in (1.25cm) from where you'll begin quilting, then use the point of the needle to gently open up the fibres of the fabric around the knot to make a small hole.

2 Tug the thread to pop the knot in between the layers of quilt sandwich. If the hole is still noticeable, use the tip of the needle to feather and close the fibres.

3 Make a running stitch through all the layers. To speed up the process, feed a few stitches at a time onto the needle. The stitches can be any length you like, but I'd avoid making them more than ⅜in (1cm) long as they may catch. I've left the gap in between the stitches smaller than the stitches themselves, but you could have them evenly spaced. Practise on some spare fabric first to see what kind of look you like.

4 I've simply outlined the pink squares on my quilt, but use templates or marking tools (see pages 22 and 23) if you wish.

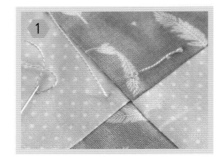

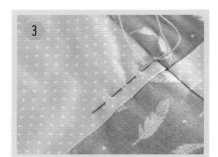

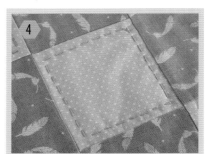

Don't worry about the stitches being perfectly even; I think big stitch quilting lends itself to the hand-made look!

84

REVERSE APPLIQUÉ MESSENGER BAG

Techniques

- ⊕ Reverse appliqué
- ⊕ Hand quilting
- ⊕ Big stitch quilting
- ⊕ Bag making

You will need

- ⊕ 20in (51cm) square piece of outer fabric
- ⊕ 20in (51cm) square piece of lining fabric
- ⊕ 20in (51cm) square piece of fusible fleece
- ⊕ 40 x 2in (102 x 5cm) strip of fabric, for the strap
- ⊕ Five 12 x 2in (30.5 x 5cm) strips of different-patterned fabric, for the appliqué
- ⊕ 8 x 16in (20.5 x 40.75cm) piece of inexpensive fabric: I used calico
- ⊕ Embroidery thread/floss and needle
- ⊕ Two 1in (2.5cm) rectangular rings
- ⊕ Two ½in (13mm) swivel snap clasps
- ⊕ Magnetic snap
- ⊕ Erasable marker pen and ruler
- ⊕ Heart template (see page 93)
- ⊕ **Optional:** strong wet fabric glue

Finished size

8 x 10 x 1½in (20.5 x 25.5 x 4cm)

Notes

Use a ¼in (5mm) seam allowance.

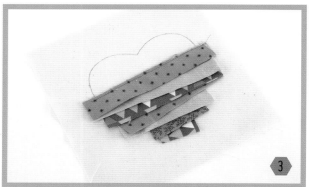

1 Cut one 9½ x 18in (24.25 x 45.75cm) piece and one 9½in (24.25cm) square from both the outer and lining fabrics. Iron fusible fleece to the wrong sides of the outer pieces and trim.

2 Cut your calico into two 8in (20.5cm) squares then use the heart template to draw a heart at the centre of each.

3 Fold your fabric strips in half lengthways, wrong sides together, and press. Starting at the bottom of one of the hearts, sew the strips over the top, overlapping them and at slight angles to each other, until the heart shape is covered.

4 Place the second heart fabric piece centrally onto one long outer bag panel, right sides together, with the bottom point of the heart sitting 1in (2.5cm) from the bottom edge of the fabric. This piece will fold over to make the bag flap. Be aware that if you're using a fabric with a directional print, you'll need the fabric to be the right way round when the flap is folded over! Sew around the heart using a small stitch length on your machine. A little tip: when you come to sew the 'V' shape at the top of the heart, take a couple of stitches straight across the point instead of pivoting – you'll find the point will sit flatter when turned.

5 Cut out the centre of the heart, close to the stitches. Snip into the curves and the top 'V' of the heart and snip off the bottom point. Push the calico through the hole and press.

6 Pin the calico with the strips of fabric behind the heart aperture. Sew around the heart by hand with a running stitch (you could machine sew, if you prefer), as shown. Using a circular template or ribbon reel, round off the bottom corners of the flap piece.

7 Starting 1¼in (3.25cm) from one side of the outer bag panel, draw lines across the fabric that are 1in (2.5cm) apart with your erasable marker pen. Hand-sew running stitch along these lines.

8 Apply the larger half of the magnetic snap centrally to the right side of the outer bag panel, 4½in (11cm) down from the top. The second half is placed centrally to the right side of the larger lining piece, 1¼in (3.25cm) from the top.

9 Cut a ¾in (2cm) square from the bottom of each piece of fabric.

10 Sew the lining pieces right sides together, leaving the cut-out corners unsewn and a turning gap in the bottom seam of about 4in (10cm). Pinch the cut-out corners so that the side seams sit over the base seam, and sew straight across to make the bag base square, as shown. Repeat with the outer bag, this time without the turning gap. Round off the corners of the flap lining using your circle template.

11 Cut two 3in (7.5cm) lengths from the strap fabric. Fold the long edges to the centre and press, then fold in half and press again. Top-stitch along either side.

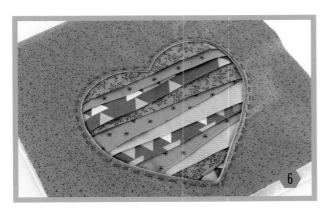

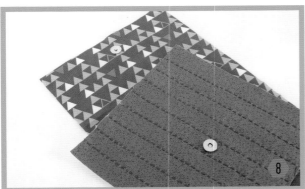

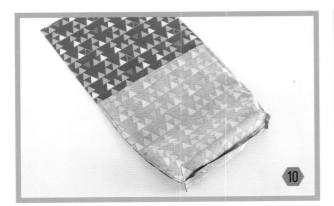

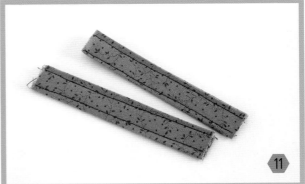

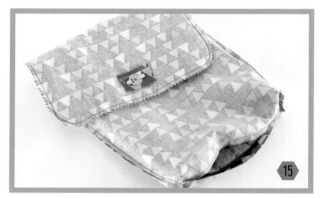

12 With the remaining strap fabric, fold the long edges to the centre then in half again and press. Turn the folded edges back on themselves to expose the raw edges, then sew straight across the ends.

13 Fold the ends back in again to conceal the raw edges and end seams then top-stitch all the way around. Thread each end through a swivel snap and sew across to secure.

14 Thread each shorter 3in (7.5cm) strap through a rectangular ring, tucking the raw ends underneath. Sew the ringed straps over each side seam, 1in (2.5cm) down from the top of the bag (you may find it easier to pop a little wet glue under the strap to hold it in place before sewing) – stitch in a square shape to attach the straps, as this will make a stronger seam.

15 Drop the outer bag inside the lining, right sides facing and matching the seams. Sew all around the top of the bag and flap, then snip around the curves and into the corners – to make this easier, I used pinking shears.

16 Turn the bag right side out through the gap in the lining, then machine sew the opening closed. Push the lining inside the bag and press.

17 Hand-sew a running stitch all around the top of the bag and the flap. Clip on the strap to finish.

TYING YOUR QUILT

Tying adds a touch of vintage charm to your quilt, particularly when the project has been hand-made. The three layers in your quilt sandwich are literally tied together, from the top through to the backing, to secure them in place. It's a quick and simple way of quilting, but take care when washing as this method isn't as secure as machine quilting. You can use strong thread, embroidery thread/floss, knitting or crochet yarn – anything that will suit your quilt!

1 Mark the position of your ties with an erasable marker pen. These could be over an intersection or in the centre of a patch; tying at regular intervals looks best.

Tip

Don't make your ties too far apart – take a look at the manufacturer's instructions on your wadding/batting packaging for the recommended quilting distance.

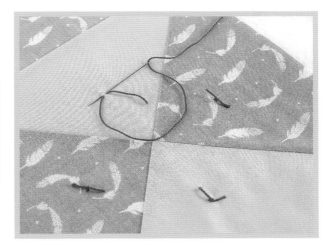

2 Thread an 18in (45.75cm) length of thread/floss or yarn onto your needle (your choice of tying material will determine what kind of needle you use). Take your needle through the marked spot from the top of the quilt, leaving a tail of about 2in (5cm).

3 Bring the needle back up again, slightly to the side of the marked spot. Go into and back out of the same spot. Tie the thread tails into a double knot and trim the ends. Repeat!

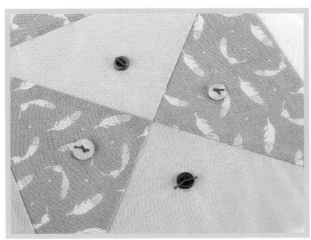

It's a bit of fun on a modern quilt to add a button to the tie, before making a double knot!

Project
HUMBUG HEXIE QUILT

Techniques

- English paper piecing
- Adding borders
- Tying your quilt
- Bias binding

Finished size

41 x 32½in (104.25 x 82.5cm)

You will need

- Six fat quarters of co-ordinating fabric
- 44 x 37in (112 x 94cm) piece of natural wadding/batting
- 44 x 37in (112 x 94cm) piece of backing fabric
- 44 x 24in (112 x 61cm) piece of co-ordinating fabric, for the borders: I chose the same fabric used for the backing
- Hexie template (see page 92) to cut three-hundred 1in (2.5cm) size hexagon paper pieces: I cut out approx. twenty paper hexagons then simply re-used them
- 4¼yd (4m) length of 1in (2.5cm) wide single-fold bias binding
- Embroidery thread/floss and needle, for tying the quilt

Notes

Use a ¼in (5mm) seam allowance.

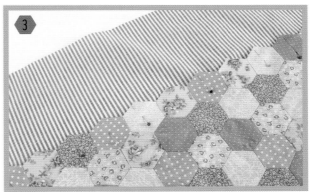

1 Prepare your fabric and hexagon paper pieces as on pages 76 and 77. As I like to re-use the papers, I wrap around twenty at a time. For my quilt I didn't want to create any particular pattern; however, I sewed the hexagon pieces together in an order that made sure two hexagon shapes of the same pattern weren't next to each other. Remove the papers from the hexagons as you go, but leave the outer papers intact.

2 Keep sewing the pieces together until your patchwork top is approximately 24 x 32in (61 x 81.25cm) in size.

3 Lay the fabric flat, making sure there are no missing pieces from the edges. Press the fabric before removing the outer paper pieces. Cut the border fabric into 6in (15.25cm) wide strips, 12in (30.5cm) longer than each patchworked side. Pin the patchworked fabric centrally over the right side of one border piece, overlapping by 1in (2.5cm). Add the three remaining borders in the same way.

4 Mitre the corners of your borders, as per page 61. Once these are in place, slip stitch along the outer edge of your hexies to secure them to the border fabric.

5 Make your quilt sandwich by adding wadding/batting then your backing fabric behind the patchwork top and tack/baste them in place – I've used fabric spray to hold the layers together. Tie your quilt layers together. I chose to tie my quilt with co-ordinating embroidery thread/ floss, and added these to every other hexie.

6 Apply bias binding (see pages 52 and 53) to finish.

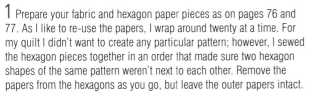

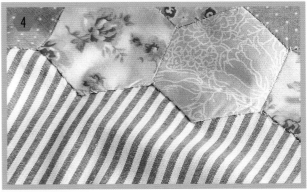

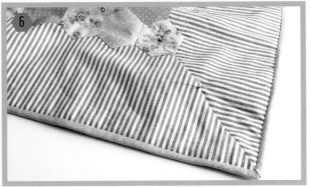

TEMPLATES

All the templates are given at actual size.
Simply trace them off.

Humbug Hexie Quilt
on page 90

CUT 20 FROM PAPER

Bunting Quilt
on page 68

CUT 35 FROM PATTERNED FABRIC,
40 FROM WHITE

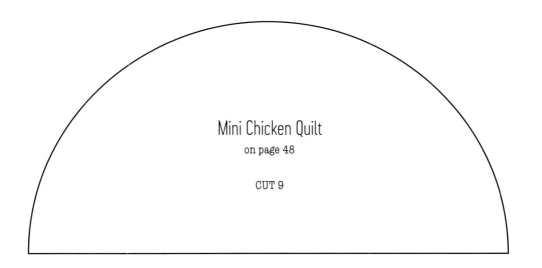

Mini Chicken Quilt
on page 48

CUT 9

Reverse Appliqué Messenger Bag
on page 85

CUT 1 FROM PAPER

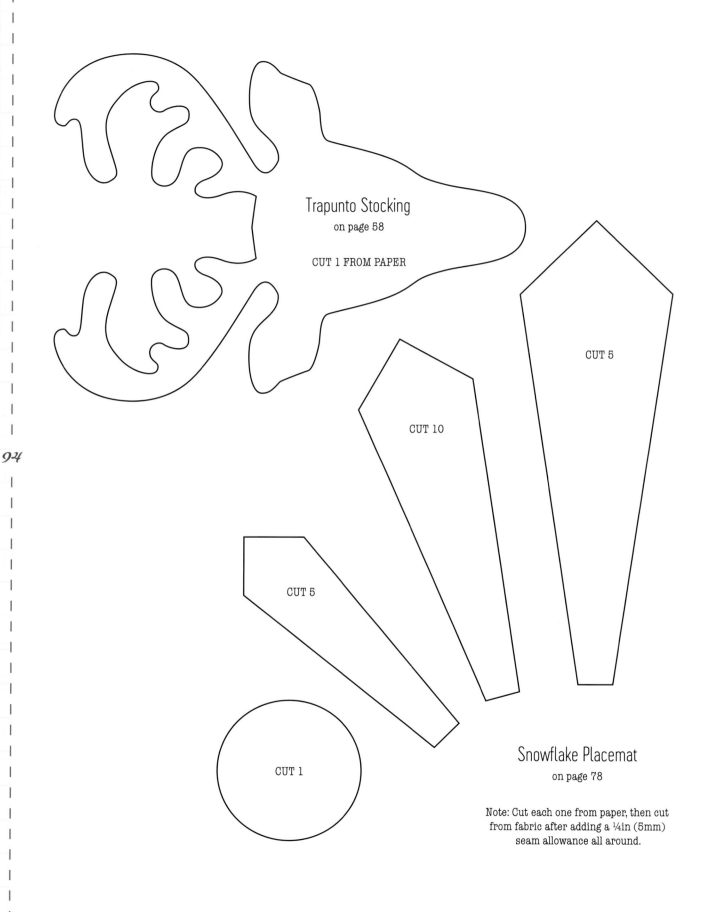

Trapunto Stocking
on page 58

CUT 1 FROM PAPER

CUT 5

CUT 10

CUT 5

CUT 5

CUT 1

Snowflake Placemat
on page 78

Note: Cut each one from paper, then cut
from fabric after adding a ¼in (5mm)
seam allowance all around.

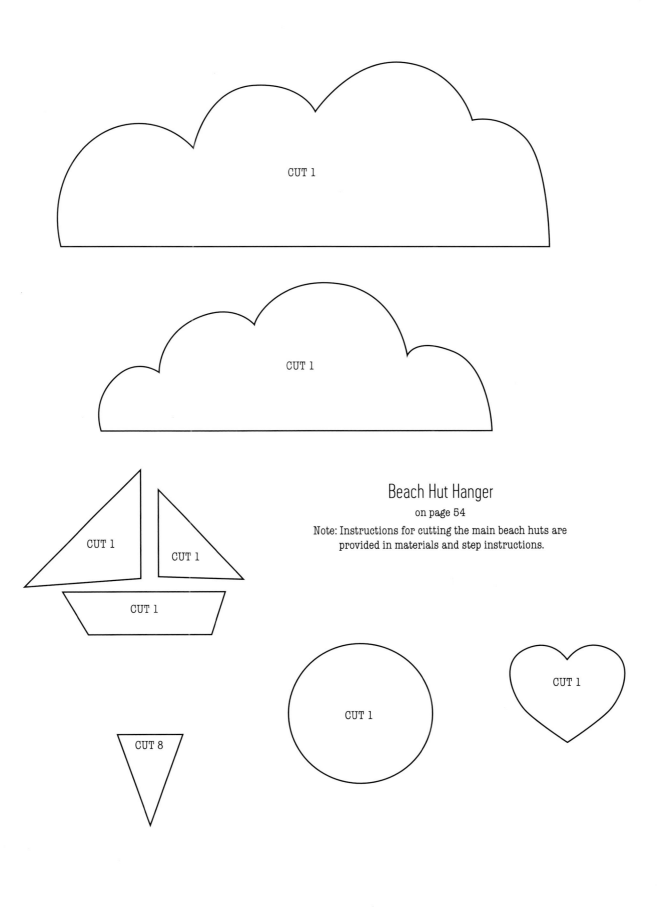

CUT 1

CUT 1

Beach Hut Hanger

on page 54

Note: Instructions for cutting the main beach huts are
provided in materials and step instructions.

CUT 1

CUT 1

CUT 1

CUT 1

CUT 1

CUT 8

INDEX